BH

Pamela and Matthew Granovetter

Forgive Me, Partner!

— the guide to a successful partnership —

**Special: 3 chapters by Larry Cohen
"On Forming a Partnership"
a start-up/refresher course**

To Order More Copies of this book, send $14.95 per copy plus $3 postage
per address (or inquire about bulk orders) to:

Granovetter Books
P.O. Box 43579
Cleveland, Ohio 44143-0579
Credit-Cards, Fax: 216 446-9537
EMAIL: Gran@Netvision.net.il

Printed in the United States of America
ISBN 0-940257-21-1

Contents

❋ Special topics ❋

Foreword

Our late friend and teacher, Victor Mitchell, used to answer partnership problems diplomatically. First one player would come to him and ask if he bid the hand correctly. And Victor would agree with him. Then the fellow's partner would take Victor aside and Victor would agree with him as well.

"They can't both be right, Victor," I once commented.

Victor thought about this and responded, "You know something — you're right, too."

The truth later came out, behind closed doors, that Victor thought both partners were wrong. Neither one catered to the needs of the other.

What your bid or play means in theory is of no use if your partner doesn't accept the theory.

This is the main philosophy of this book. In our Partnership Bridge columns from the ACBL Bulletin, we show both sides of the issue. In Part I of this book, we use the same formula, but go a bit further: We come to some conclusive middle-of-the-road agreements, which we think will be useful for all players in improving their judgment in the critical situations that arise at the table. For partnerships that hope to get off on the right foot or need a new set of guidelines to choose from, this book should provide the answers. And each of us, even those without regular partners, will benefit from the study of deals in which both sides took reasonable views, yet disaster resulted. The solutions rest in the partnership principles that follow each of our arguments. We hope you find them thought-provoking and helpful.

In the third part of this book, we offer some important guidelines and quizzes to help form a partnership (good for revamping old partnerships as well). Nevertheless, despite the importance of practice and maintaining a set of partnership notes, we believe that 75% of partnership success rides on being a good partner; the remaining 25% is system and understandings. Proof of this is — as Larry Cohen mentions in his discussion in Part II — that first-time partnerships (the very first session played by two people) have by far a fantastic average of success (and victories!) than partnerships of long-standing. During that first outing each player is prepared to do his best to be a good partner. This is how it should be even on the one-thousandth outing.

We'd like to thank a number of people for their advice and help with this book: Kathie Wei-Sender, Audrey and Martin Hoffman, and Chip Martel, who offered his own partnership understandings for the quiz and rules in Chapter 15: What Does the Last Call Mean? And special thanks to Larry Cohen for his wonderful essays (Chapters 12-14).

Pamela and Matthew Granovetter
July, 1997

This book is dedicated to:

Eve Wald

and . . .
Henry Francis and Brent Manley, the American Contract
Bridge League editors of our monthly partnership bridge
column
Pat and Jimmy Cayne
Kris Griffin
Jill Roberts
Linda and Ralph Simpson

and Rita Rand, a good friend
and good partner

— In memory of Alfred Sheinwold 1912-1997 —

Part I

Nine Ways to Help Partner

— scenes from a married partnership —

Introduction

Here's another Vic Mitchell story: This guy comes over to Vic and says, "I really played great, Vic. You have no idea. Every bid, every card, was perfection. Even my opponents complimented me."

"Eh, well, sounds great. How'd you do?"

"Oh, we were below average, but my partner wasn't exactly at the top of his game, if you know what I mean."

"Yeah, well, 'I love me — I think I'm grand.'"

"Whad'ya mean?"

"I mean you played great. I can't wait to play against ya."

Still another Vic story: Victor was playing bridge with a student who was having a heart problem. And sitting across from the master in a two-session regional was not going to help matters.

"Are you all right?" asked Vic.

"To tell you the truth, I'm a bit nervous."

On the first board the bidding goes one spade on Vic's left, pass, two hearts on Vic's right. Vul against not, Vic steps in with three diamonds. Vic has five diamonds to the king and about seven points. LHO starts to think and looks at Victor in bewilderment (i.e., Did Vic really stick his neck out on the chopping block?)

"Oh, my God," says Vic, "whad'd I do?" (This is Vic's subtle way of helping LHO.)

"Double" say lefty. All pass, down five, minus 1400.

"Sorry," says Vic to his partner. "I ruined it for us. We ain't got a chance in holy hell now."

"That's all right," says his partner, smiling and more relaxed. They went on to win the section.

* * *

Helping partner to play his best is a critical part of the game. Most of us overlook the mathematical percentages of how well we are performing. For example, if you are playing at 90% of your potential and partner is playing at 50%, what do you have? An average of 70%. These percentages are vital when weighed against the percentages of your opponents.

Let's say that Joe and Sally, two average players, are playing against Nick and Dick, two bridge stars. Let's assume that Nick and Dick are twice as good (that's a lot) as Joe and Sally, when everyone plays his best. Now let's say that on this particular day, Nick and Dick are playing below par, at an average of 40% of their ability. If Joe and Sally can play at 80% of their ability or better, they are suddenly the favorites. If Joe and Sally can play at 70% and have 20% more luck, they can still beat Nick and Dick, who on average play twice as well as they do!

This is not an uncommon scenario. We've seen how great bridge teams are sometimes upset in early rounds of knock-out team events; or how one day the "worst player" in the club cleans up at the rubber bridge table. In fact, the "superstars" all have their bad days. It's up to the rest of us to take advantage of these opportunities.

Now you can see the importance of playing at your highest potential and getting partner to do the same. As we saw in Vic's story about the man who had a heart problem, there are times when helping partner reach his potential is the most vital task at hand.

> The most important way to help partner is by keeping cool when the wheels come off — especially when the hand is not yet over. . . .

Chapter 1: When Dummy Comes Down

Pamela: A few years ago, I learned the lesson of a lifetime during a Vanderbilt match, and I was the dummy! Matthew and I were on a team with Steve Weinstein and Fred Stewart. We went into the last 16 boards of a 64-board match down 60 imps against a team of world champions. The odds of our making a comeback were astronomical. We had to hope for wild deals, and the one thing we had to do was bid every reasonable game contract in sight and hope it made. At least this should have been our strategy. But look at this deal. I will give it to you from my husband's position. You pick up, vul against not, in third position:

♠ Q 4   ♡ A 2   ◇ Q J 10 9 8 6 3   ♣ K 10

Two passes to you and you have your first decision to make. You could open the bidding one diamond, two diamonds (weak two-bid), or three diamonds (a preempt).

There's much to be said for all three bids in third position. The two extremes are tempting: The three-bid gives the biggest headache to the opponents, but the one-bid gives you the best chance to reach a notrump game if partner has a maximum pass and a diamond honor. My husband chose the middle road, the weak two-bid, which I do not disagree with. Without the majors, you want to raise the level of bidding room of the opponents, but you don't want to put all your eggs in one basket, and two diamonds leaves bidding room for your side as well.

Over two diamonds, your LHO doubles for takeout. Partner

passes and your RHO bid two hearts. Now it is back to you again:

♠ Q 4   ♡ A 2   ◇ Q J 10 9 8 6 3   ♣ K 10

West	Pamela	East	You
—	pass	pass	2 ◇
double	pass	2 ♡	?

You are probably a little sorry now that you didn't start with three diamonds. Nevertheless, you can bid it now if you like, although you are breaking the "golden rule" of never bidding again after a preempt. What would you do? Pass or bid three diamonds?

Suppose you bid three diamonds. And, once again, I don't disagree. The golden rule of never bidding again after making a preempt is a nice rule, but it never made sense to me. If your preempt is strange in some way (like this two-diamond opening) surely you are entitled to describe your hand more. Besides, in this case, down 60 imps, you can't expect to pick up points by sitting in your chair like a mummy.

Continuing with the auction, over your three diamonds, lefty passes and partner suddenly springs to life with a cuebid of three hearts:

West	Pamela	East	You
—	pass	pass	2 ◇
double	pass	2 ♡	3 ◇
pass	3 ♡	pass	?

Suddenly you have a third decision to make. But first analyze partner's bid. If her bid is asking for a heart stopper for three notrump, maybe you should bid it. If partner is merely expressing a great hand for diamonds, maybe you should consider a jump to five diamonds. Or maybe you can hedge by bidding something in between.

Your choices are: three spades, three notrump, four clubs, four diamonds, and five diamonds. Decide before you turn the page.

> **Note:** Third position is the "seat of sin." All opening bids in this position are tainted. You might open one of a suit for the lead or a weak two-bid on a five-card suit or a three-bid with two outside honors! Partner, who's passed in first position, must always allow for these possibilities.

 The delayed raise

What does it mean when partner passes over a takeout double and later comes into the auction? The bidding on this deal can cause you to scratch your head in disbelief, unless you have some understanding of the matter. Why didn't Pamela raise to three diamonds directly?

The answer is this: She must have good defensive values. If she did not hold defensive values, she would have raised immediately. One way to lose a partner is to pass his preempt and then later back in. The best strategy is to raise immediately or forever hold your peace, *unless you have strong defensive values, i.e., you want the opponents to get too high.*

What would a redouble have meant over West's double? This is a matter of partnership agreement. We play redouble to mean: "Let's double them, if we can." Others play redouble to mean: "Help! Let's get out of this contract!"

A further consideration is the bid of 2NT after a takeout double. This is usually played as a game try with a fit for partner. But Pamela was a passed hand, so both the redouble and 2NT responses were unlikely calls.

If you bid anything but three notrump, take a demerit. If you bid five diamonds, take two demerits. This was the full deal:

North dealer   North (Pamela)
N-S vul
                ♠ A 10 6 5
                ♡ J 6 3
                ◇ A 2
                ♣ Q J 7 3

West   East
♠ K J 7 3   ♠ 9 8 2
♡ K Q 9 5   ♡ 10 8 7 4
◇ 5 4   ◇ K 7
♣ A 9 8   ♣ 6 5 4 2

                South (Matthew)
                ♠ Q 4
                ♡ A 2
                ◇ Q J 10 9 8 6 3
                ♣ K 10

	Pamela		Matthew
West	North	East	South
—	pass	pass	2 ◇
double	pass	2 ♡	3 ◇
pass	3 ♡	pass	4 ◇
(all pass)			

Opening lead: ♡K

I passed my 12-point hand because I knew the player at the other table would open my hand, and by passing I would create a swing. Matthew opened 2◇ for similar reasons. He was a jack heavy for his bid, but he wanted to create a different auction from the other table. These tactics are necessary when you are far behind in a match and make better strategy than wild bidding or psyching.

After West made a takeout double, I decided to pass and judge what to do later. The pass of a takeout double with a good hand can be quite lucrative when the opponents fall into the trap of thinking they have more than they really have.

I was surprised to hear Matthew bid again by himself, but I understood his three-diamond bid to mean that he had a seven-card suit and a maximum weak two. Now my hand was strong enough to try for nine tricks. I just needed a heart stopper from partner. So I cuebid three hearts, asking Matthew to bid three notrump with a stopper there.

As you can see, however, he bid four diamonds, even though he had a heart stopper.

West led the ♡K. When Matthew won the first trick with the ♡A, I looked at him in amazement. He started to mutter an excuse. This quickly turned into an argument, in the course of which he failed to study the hand before playing to the next trick. While arguing with me, he led the ♢Q for a finesse. East won the trick and shifted to a spade. The defense now had four tricks and Matthew had suddenly gone down in a cold, simple hand. He should have led back a heart or the ♣K at trick two — there's nothing to it.

Still, it was my fault. I never should have distracted him by showing emotion at the table. When he started muttering, I should have let him mutter.

Matthew: I'm not sure which came first, your stare or my muttering. Nevertheless, it's very noble of you to take the blame. But I beg to differ with you on two points. First, the calamity was my fault completely. I am certainly experienced enough to forget the errors of the bidding when dummy comes down, and concentrate on the play. It was the frustration of the circumstances that led me to argue at the table. Here we were in a partscore, cold for a game, when it was our main strategy at this point in the match to stretch to game contracts.

That brings me to my second point. What did your pass followed

North dealer North (Pamela)
N-S vul
             ♠ A 10 6 5
             ♡ J 6 3
             ◊ A 2
             ♣ Q J 7 3

West   East
♠ K J 7 3   ♠ 9 8 2
♡ K Q 9 5   ♡ 10 8 7 4
◊ 5 4   ◊ K 7
♣ A 9 8   ♣ 6 5 4 2

           South (Matthew)
             ♠ Q 4
             ♡ A 2
             ◊ Q J 10 9 8 6 3
             ♣ K 10

	Pamela		Matthew
West	North	East	South
—	pass	pass	2 ◊
double	pass	2 ♡	3 ◊
pass	3 ♡	pass	4 ◊
(all pass)			

Opening lead: ♡K

by a cuebid mean? You say you were trapping when you passed. But why trap with a weak heart holding? Now take the ◊A and put it into the heart suit and you have a nice trap pass. But you had honor and one in my suit. Why not raise immediately?

When you passed and later backed in with a cuebid over my three-diamond call, I assumed you were unlikely to hold a diamond honor. It was clear that you didn't hold both the ace and king of diamonds, and you also didn't hold both a diamond honor and a heart stopper, or you would have bid three notrump yourself — you wouldn't have asked me to bid it.

On that analysis, you could not possibly hold a hand where I could make three notrump. The reason my analysis turned out wrong was that you had a diamond honor and, more important, you miraculously provided a second heart stopper with your jack-third. Even with the hand you held, we only have to split the opponents' heart honors to make three notrump a hopeless contract. My four-diamond bid was, therefore, extremely fine-tuned. Imagine my frustration when West led the ♡K. Can you blame me for muttering?

Pamela: Yes, perhaps I should have raised directly, but there you go again trying to fine tune an auction in the middle of a thunderstorm. When you're down 60 imps, don't get scientific! Just close your eyes and bid game. Let me tell the readers the rest of the story.

When our teammates rushed out to compare scores with glowing hope on their faces (they had a great game in the other room), I wanted to die. I knew we had had our chances (because we also had some good results) but had blown it all on this deal. When we totaled the scores, I was in shock to learn we had won back 59 imps — one short. I was ready for suicide or murder, whichever was easier. Then, thank God, when we did not hear a victory scream from the other team comparing scores on the other side of the hallway, we realized something was afoot. Yes, we had scored a hand incorrectly and had picked up 60 imps, not 59. So we had an eight-board playoff and we actually went on to win the match.

In the cool aftermath, we can now analyze this deal. At the other table, the North-South players bid to three notrump from the North side, and our teammates defended well by leading a heart through the ace and continuing the suit. They took three hearts, a diamond, and the ♣A to defeat the contract one trick, making the result a push. Had we bid three notrump from the South side, we would have won 12 imps to clinch the match. But had I just remained poised as dummy in four diamonds, my husband would have made the contract and we also would have clinched the match.

Partnership Principles

• When partner puts the dummy down, keep quiet and play the hand calmly. The bidding is history.

• Don't watch partner play the hand! This is difficult for dummy, but rewarding. If you don't watch, you'll have nothing to say and you won't be steaming or thinking about how *you* would have played the hand better. Also, this rule can be a lifesaver in long tournaments, where it is so easy to tire in the late rounds.

• In a team match, you never know what's going on at the other table. If you are far behind, always assume that your partners are doing sensationally and play accordingly. If you are far ahead, assume your partners are have a disastrous set, and be careful.

• The way to win back 60 imps is to bid and play *slightly* differently than the other table, and be right. If you recklessly bid *every* hand to game, some contracts will be hopeless, and you'll lose back half of what you've gained on your successes.

❋ After a blunder ❋

Pamela: What do you say to partner after he makes an obvious blunder on defense? Saying nothing (along with a cold stare) can sometimes be worse than making a remark.

Matthew: When I used to play with Sam Stayman, and I made an error, he used to say: "Matt, was there anything I could have done to help you?" Unfortunately, I heard it too many times.

Pamela: Perhaps a cold silence isn't so bad, but I think a warm, encouraging word is the best compromise.

Note: The absolutely worst thing a player can do is denigrate his partner in front of others (or to others). Unfortunately, we hear all too often: "Hey, look what my partner did to me this time."

Chapter 2: What is Partner Doing?

Matthew: I'm the last guy in the world to complain about too many gadgets. But when I receive a treatise in the mail entitled "243 minor treatments and conventions," I begin to sweat. All this for one date at the local bridge club! I study and study and study. Finally the big night arrives. Before I can get comfortable in my seat, he opens one diamond and I have:

♠ 5 4 2 ♡ 5 4 3 ◇ A K J 9 6 4 ♣ A

I try to remember our minor-suit agreements. A single raise is 5-9 — that's no good. A jump to the three level is a limit raise. That's no good. Hmm, this is a bit ridiculous. We have 243 treatments and conventions and I can't make a forcing raise in my partner's opening-bid suit. So what can I respond?

My choices are a bit weird. I could bid one heart (or one spade for that matter) and hope to get back to diamonds later. I suppose two clubs is a possibility, though this is getting eccentric. Other than these responses, I might try a simple four diamonds or even five diamonds. Of course, three notrump would be lost, so I guess that's my final option. The choices are: one heart, one spade, two clubs, four diamonds, five diamonds, and three notrump. Looks like election day with no one to vote for. What would you choose?

At the table, I closed my eyes (figuratively speaking) and responded one heart. If I was going to lie about a major, it might as well be hearts, and I couldn't stomach responding in a singleton (two clubs). The raise to four diamonds is generally some kind of preempt, so I was left with five diamonds, three notrump and one heart. The first two bids were just too committal on the first round of the auction, which is why I chose one heart. But it was not a success.

North dealer	North (new partner)
None vul	♠ 3
	♡ A Q 10 6
	◇ Q 10 8 5 3 2
	♣ K Q

West	East
♠ A K Q 10 9	♠ J 8 7 6
♡ K J 9	♡ 8 7 2
◇ —	◇ 7
♣ J 10 8 5 3	♣ 9 7 6 4 2

South (Matthew)
♠ 5 4 2
♡ 5 4 3
◇ A K J 9 6 4
♣ A

West	North	East	South
—	1 ◇	pass	1 ♡
2 NT	3 ♣	3 ♠	4 ◇
4 ♠	4 NT	pass	5 ♣
pass	5 ♡	pass	6 ◇
pass	7 ♡	(all pass)	

Opening lead: ♠A

Matthew: I'll try to translate the auction. West's bid of two notrump was for the black suits and my partner's cuebid was a game try in hearts. He thought he had too much just to bid three hearts.

When East bid three spades, I bid four diamonds. I knew it was futile to raise his diamonds, because he was obviously coming in hearts, but maybe, just maybe I could convince him I had diamonds and only diamonds from here to Canarsie if I bid four diamonds and then corrected his four-heart correction to five diamonds.

West's four spades didn't help us. My partner bid Blackwood and this was quite disturbing. First of all, I could no longer rebid diamonds naturally. If I responded five diamonds, it would be a Blackwood response, and six diamonds would show a void in diamonds. Nevertheless, here is where my conscientious studying of "the notes" showed advantage. I recognized this particular Blackwood as "1430 Keycard Blackwood" for hearts. The number "1430" means that my five-club and five-diamond responses are reverse (five clubs would show one or four keycards and five diamonds zero or three). Thus, if I bid five clubs (1 or 4), there would be a 50% chance that he'd bid five diamonds as a relay asking me for the queen of hearts! Whereupon I could pass.

So I tried five clubs, but he confounded me with five hearts. He held only one keycard and was signing off in game. At this point, I might have passed. But when I thought about it, it made no sense. After all, we were off only one ace and it was clear to me that we would have an equal if not better play in six diamonds than in the stupid contract of five hearts.

So I retreat to six diamonds and he alerts. Whereupon I resist the temptation to kick him under the table, although by now I've given up on ever partnering him again. In the meantime, he leaps to seven hearts. Then he explains that I have shown four key cards and the ◇K for my continuation to six diamonds.

West places the ♠A on the table and my partner looks at it in dismay, mumbling something about page 79 of the notes. After a few miracles I end up down only one.

Pamela: Somehow I feel this could only happen to you. But the truth is that your experience is not uncommon. Experts (or should

North dealer   North (new partner)
None vul   ♠ 3
                ♡ A Q 10 6
                ◇ Q 10 8 5 3 2
                ♣ K Q

West   East
♠ A K Q 10 9   ♠ J 8 7 6
♡ K J 9   ♡ 8 7 2
◇ —   ◇ 7
♣ J 10 8 5 3   ♣ 9 7 6 4 2

                South (Matthew)
                ♠ 5 4 2
                ♡ 5 4 3
                ◇ A K J 9 6 4
                ♣ A

West	North	East	South
—	1 ◇	pass	1 ♡
2 NT	3 ♣	3 ♠	4 ◇
4 ♠	4 NT	pass	5 ♣
pass	5 ♡	pass	6 ◇
pass	7 ♡	(all pass)	

Opening lead: ♠A

I say pseudo-experts?) often paint themselves into a corner by making artificial bid after artificial bid when an unsophisticated, natural jump would have done the job. It's difficult to pick the worst bid in your auction, but if I had to be completely fair, I'd choose your one-heart response. I would never agree to play without a forcing raise.

Matthew: Hey, I'm not the first guy to use limit raises in the minors. This is a very popular method. Let's suppose you were in my shoes and had to play without a forcing raise. What would you have done?

Pamela: In most of my rubber bridge games, South would solve the problem by taking a shot at six diamonds, hoping for some good luck or the wrong opening lead. But I suppose five diamonds is a more sensible call.

Matthew: Yes, but this wasn't rubber bridge; it was duplicate. I couldn't afford to go past 3NT, if that was our spot. Let me put it this way: A gun is put to your head and you must decide between one heart, one spade and two clubs. What would you bid?

Pamela: OK, if I had to choose among your ghastly choices, I think I would have responded two clubs. At least then no matter how many clubs he bid, I could always correct to diamonds.

Matthew: That's a good idea. Bid the suit under his suit. Nevertheless, I think if you play limit raises, the remedy is to play some additional bids that are carefully coded as forcing raises. For example, a method that is gaining popularity is "Criss-cross." The jump shift to the other minor shows a forcing raise in opener's minor.

Pamela: A better remedy is to limit the size of your convention card. Artificial sequences that come up once every five years are a burden to a partnership. Unless you're part of a professional pair that talks bridge every day, you should keep your convention card natural and practical.

Partnership Principles

• Make sure you have in your repertoire a forcing response to partner's opening-bid suit.

• If you ever find yourself stuck for a forcing bid, try to bid a short minor rather than a short major. It is always preferable to lie about a minor than a major. Maybe that's why they're called minors.

• Never agree to play a set of notes in a new partnership (until you have played together a few times). Simply fill out a convention card and keep discussion to a minimum. This is true even if you are planning to enter what you consider to be an important event. One of the reasons that first-time partnerships have a high record of success is that *they keep things simple.*

Chapter 3: White Lies

Matthew: Breaking agreements that you've made with your partner is a surefire way to destroy a partnership. If you agree to play 15-17 notrumps and open with 14, regardless of how it works on that particular hand, partner will be nervous every time you open one notrump in the future. But what about white lies? You know what I mean. Partner asks you a question in the bidding and you, for a very good reason, answer with a lie. For example, you've overbid in the auction, and when partner asks for aces, you show one ace when you have two. On the surface, partners don't like this and they quickly start looking around the room for a new one when this happens.

On the other side of the coin, however, partners appreciate it when you correct an earlier mistake but not when you compound one, even if it means you're telling the truth. Let's look at two examples and see if we can come to any constructive conclusions.

The first problem occurred in a tournament in Bombay, India. Your partner is Jaggy Shivdasani, one of India's finest players. You hold:

♠ Q 10 5 4 ♡ 2 ◇ 9 6 5 ♣ Q J 7 5 2

All vulnerable, your partner opens the bidding one heart and it goes pass on your right. Do you respond one spade or do you pass?

There are two philosophies here. The more traditional is to pass, before it gets worse. Respond one spade, says the pessimist, and the next thing you'll hear is three hearts. The optimist, however, responds one spade to improve the contract. This more modern approach balances the small loss of getting overboard with a tremendous gain when partner raises spades to game or rebids clubs!

Therefore, let's say you respond one spade, as the player in Bombay did. The next hand passes and partner jump-rebids to three diamonds — not exactly what you had been hoping for. You were planning, of course, to pass his next bid, but suddenly a partnership issue is at stake: He has made a forcing bid and expects to hear from you again. The question is: Do you pass or do you bid three notrump, your only reasonable alternative?

In answer to this, here is our man in Bombay, Jaggy.

Jaggy: Bridge is a strange game. You go through all sorts of emotions: joy, exaltation, depression, anger, violence. On the hand

 How light do you respond?

"The Book" says you need 6 or more points to respond at the one level.

We also like to respond at favorable vulnerability with a yarborough! This makes it more difficult for fourth hand to enter the auction and may prevent the opponents from reaching game. But it has its risks. Partner may have extra strength and rebid too high.

Another idea is to respond whenever you have a long major, and another is to respond whenever you hold an ace.

Before you try any of these ideas, agree with your partner, so he won't be upset when he sees your dummy.

that was presented to you, I experienced a new one: the feeling of loneliness. I was dropped in the middle of a well. Here was the full deal:

```
South dealer      North
N-S vul           ♠ Q 10 5 4
                  ♡ 2
                  ◊ 9 6 5
                  ♣ Q J 7 5 2

West                                    East
♠ 3 2                                   ♠ J 9 8
♡ K 6 4 3                               ♡ Q 10 8
◊ K 10 3                                ◊ Q 8 7 2
♣ 9 8 4 3                               ♣ K 10 6

                  South (Jaggy)
                  ♠ A K 7 6
                  ♡ A J 9 7 5
                  ◊ A J 4
                  ♣ A
```

Jaggy

South	West	North	East
1 ♡	pass	1 ♠	pass
3 ◊	pass	pass!	pass

Opening lead: ♣9

Jaggy: My hand was too good to make a splinter bid in clubs, so I jump-shifted with the intention of making an even stronger slam try in spades. Horror of horrors, my partner dropped me in three diamonds.

I made the contract by scrambling nine tricks on a cross ruff, but so what? We still lost 11 imps because the North-South pair at the other table bid and made four spades.

Pamela: When these things happen to me I don't feel lonely, I feel the urge to quit bridge. Once you choose to respond with a minimum, you must carry on over a forcing bid. Your partner should have rebid three notrump.

Matthew: I'm not so sure about this. Haven't you ever made a bid, then changed your mind? Let's look again at the hand Jaggy's partner held. He took a chance over one heart to improve the contract, hoping perhaps to reach a four-spade game if Jaggy could raise him. When he heard the jump shift, the poor fellow knew he could have buried the auction back at one heart, so he decided enough was enough. The chance of making three notrump on a misfit had to be small. Indeed, take one of Jaggy's spades and put it into the diamond suit. Then see what the hand makes.

Now I agree, there was a chance that Jaggy was coming in spades when he jump-shifted, but was it likely? With four spades, Jaggy might have raised directly to game or splintered. It was, therefore, quite unlikely to find Jaggy with four spades. Thus, the pass of three diamonds could be considered a percentage action in North's mind, and certainly not cause for loneliness or despair on the part of South.

Pamela: You might be right in a rubber bridge game, where partnership harmony is not a major concern, where the next deal you will be facing a new partner anyway. But when you're playing with a regular partner, and go out of the way to invite her to the ball, then leave her standing in the corner all evening, how do you think she feels?

Jaggy: Well said. Bridge is a partnership game from beginning to end. When you make a bid, you should think ahead and anticipate how the auction might develop. Don't make a bid on a whim, then drop partner in a forcing auction because you chicken out.

Matthew: Our second problem comes from a Bridge Today Magazine All-Star Game, in which 19 world champions and I competed in a round-robin Individual. In this event, everybody was required to play the same system, natural, five-card majors. Each player partnered the other 19 players for three boards. It was great fun and an important element was your knowledge of the players. I failed miserably in this department when I partnered the famous Dallas Ace, Bobby Wolff. I invite the reader to take my seat.

You pick up:

♠ K 8 6 5   ♡ J 10 4   ◇ Q J 10 3   ♣ A K

You open the bidding one diamond and Wolff responds two clubs. This particular beginning is somewhat of a controversial area in bidding theory. What should you rebid with a minimum hand? Two diamonds or two notrump? Can you reverse after a two-over-one without describing extra values? Can you rebid two notrump with one of the majors unstopped? Can you rebid two diamonds on a four-card suit, if you don't like the other alternatives?

Unless you've discussed these ideas with your partner (and how many of us have?), you must decide at the table. On this particular deal, I was the player behind these cards and I chose to rebid two spades, hoping partner would not take it as a reverse. I was unwilling to rebid two notrump without a heart stopper and equally appalled at the idea of rebidding a four-card suit. My partner next bid three diamonds, which I understood as forcing. The reason three diamonds was forcing is that he had no other way to raise diamonds at this point below the level of three notrump (the likely resting place when we do not hold a major-suit fit). Besides, there was always the chance that he thought my two-spade rebid was a reverse, and then his three-diamond bid would surely be forcing.

At this point, however, I had nowhere pleasant to go. Having shown diamonds and spades, I could not very well rebid three notrump with jack-ten-third of hearts. But I certainly had no interest in continuing toward a five-diamond contract with my balanced minimum. So I decided to bid three hearts. I meant this as a fourth-suit-forcing call, asking partner to bid three notrump if he could stop hearts. Unfortunately, my partner did not read it this way. I knew that as soon as he jumped to four notrump, Blackwood.

I now dutifully bid five diamonds, one ace, but I was beginning to wonder if I should backtrack (i.e., lie). It was obvious that Wolff had interpreted my bidding as: (1) a reverse in spades and (2) a cuebid in hearts. The next thing I heard was five notrump, asking for kings. Good grief, he was heading toward a grand slam!

Let's review:

Lamb	Wolff
1 ◇	2 ♣
2 ♠	3 ◇
3 ♡	4 NT
5 ◇	5 NT
?	

At this point, lying about my two kings was a very reasonable option, I thought. But on the other side of the coin, what if partner had all the highcards and was not relying on my questionable bidding? What if by lying, we miss the grand slam? How can I justify lying about Blackwood to one of the best players in the world?

Well, readers, what would you do? Would you lie or tell the truth? Would you rebid six hearts to show two kings or six diamonds, one king? Decide before turning the page.

South dealer   North (Wolff)
E-W vul   ♠ A 4
                  ♡ A K 2
                  ◊ A 8 5 2
                  ♣ J 7 4 3

West   East
♠ Q 10 7   ♠ J 9 3 2
♡ 8 7 5   ♡ Q 9 6 3
◊ K   ◊ 9 7 6 4
♣ 10 9 8 6 5 2   ♣ Q

                  South (Matthew)
                  ♠ K 8 6 5
                  ♡ J 10 4
                  ◊ Q J 10 3
                  ♣ A K

South	West	North	East
1 ◊	pass	2 ♣	pass
2 ♠	pass	3 ◊	pass
3 ♡	pass	4 NT	pass
5 ◊	pass	5 NT	pass
6 ♡	pass	7 ◊	(all pass)

Matthew: As you can see, it was definitely right to lie about kings (it was probably right to lie about aces on the round before). Seven diamonds was a terrible contract, even six wasn't so good, but it would have made. The point is that partner had misinterpreted my calls (or my calls were off-the-wall — choose either explanation), and it was so obvious that I think I made a terrible boner by not lying in my responses to Blackwood.

Pamela: I must say, you do get yourself into the most awful pickles. Your problem on this hand started when you were bidding by yourself instead of in a partnership. It wasn't important what you thought your bids meant as much as what partner thought your bids meant. To be successful, you must cater to your partner.

After Wolff's two-club response, you should simply have rebid two notrump, even with the weak heart holding. You knew that he was used to playing a strong-club system and that the rebid of two notrump in his book was a minimum balanced hand. Therefore, that was the practical bid. I agree, it may have backfired, if Wolff had something like ace-doubleton of hearts and three notrump was better from his side. But what was the chance of that specific holding and scenario? You had to weigh that against the simplicity and clarity of a two-notrump rebid.

Matthew: OK, OK, but what if while I was catering to his thinking, he was catering to my thinking?

Pamela: Nobody ever has or ever will cater to your thinking, dear.

Matthew: Fair enough, but what about after I had mucked it up and now had to decide between showing my aces and kings or lying about them? What would you have done in my shoes?

Pamela: I would have shown my ace, dear, as you did. But never, ever, would I have been dumb enough to show both kings. To lie about aces is a real no-no; aces are simply too important in the scheme of things. But kings is another story. The difference between game and slam is much greater than the difference between slam and a grand slam. For one thing, the field rarely reaches a grand slam, so it's much riskier to bid seven than to bid six. And there's always the chance of a poor split to destroy what seem to be a good grand slam. Remember, you must make distinctions in bridge. When you break partnership trust at the partscore or game level, you are risking partnership deterioration for sake of a small gain. But at the grand slam level, you have much more to lose if you

are wrong, so partner may forgive you for an occasional lie in order
to save the ship.

Partnership Principles

• The guiding principle in partnership discipline is that you
keep to your agreements and never lie in response to partner's
inquiries, *unless you have good reason to judge partner is counting on you for more than you've shown and the stake is very high.*

• Thus, you never lie on an opening bid, in a partscore or at the
game level. The risk is simply not worth it.

• When choosing a rebid early in the auction, think about how
partner will interpret it — not how *you* like to play it.

• Decide with your partner if you play reverses after a two-
over-one response. The auction 1◊-pass-2♣ is especially worth
reviewing. What do opener's rebids mean?

• Don't pass a forcing bid, at any level. Even if you are right,
you will destroy partner's confidence for the future.

• Never lie about aces in response to Blackwood. Because even
if you have described a hand with more values than you actually
hold, you can never be sure partner isn't looking at a very
powerful hand himself.

• But slowing partner down by lying about kings, *if you are
confident that you have overbid your hand,* is a reasonable
action. Nevertheless, be prepared to apologize if you do miss a
grand that makes.

Chapter 4: Is That Forcing?

Matthew: It's easy to get frustrated in an obscure auction. Suddenly partner springs a new bid at you and you're not sure what it means.

Is it natural?

Is it forcing?

Do you continue on or do you pass?

Try this one. You are South.

			you
West	North	East	South
2 ♠	pass	pass	double
redouble	2 NT	pass	?

Is two notrump natural or is it takeout?

If it is natural, it certainly is not forcing.

If it is takeout, you must bid, because partner has the minors and possibly no spade stopper.

OK, here is your hand. See if it helps.

♠ K 5 ♡ 10 6 4 2 ◇ A K Q 2 ♣ J 5 4

If two notrump was natural, you certainly want to pass.

If two notrump was takeout, you certainly want to bid three diamonds.

Well, which will it be?

One idea is to use a simple principle, taught to me by Dave Mason, a leading New York player of the 60's and 70's He used to say, "When in doubt, bid."

And he's right. Over the years I've had countless disasters by passing a questionable bid, when taking action would have ensured some degree of safety. On the other hand, there is no great safety in bidding when you might get overboard, particularly when a fit has not yet been established (as in this hand).

Therefore, I'd like to find a way to reword Mason's principle to make it more effective. On this hand, it failed me. It came up in a team match, and my wife was the one who made the confusing call.

```
West dealer        North (Pamela)
All vul            ♠ Q 9 2
                   ♡ 9 7 3
                   ◇ 5 4 3
                   ♣ A K Q 6

West                              East
♠ A J 10 8 7 4                    ♠ 6 3
♡ A 8                             ♡ K Q J 5
◇ 6                               ◇ J 10 9 8 7
♣ 10 9 8 7                        ♣ 3 2

                   South (Matthew)
                   ♠ K 5
                   ♡ 10 6 4 2
                   ◇ A K Q 2
                   ♣ J 5 4
```

	Pamela		Matthew
West	North	East	South
2 ♠	pass	pass	double
redouble	2 NT	pass	3 ◇
(all pass)			

Pamela: Confusing call? What would you bid with my hand? Passing the redouble was out of the question. That would show a conversion of partner's takeout double to penalty. This is standard, and should be discussed in all partnerships, but it's another issue (see page 38).

We have never discussed this particular auction, so I assumed that any bid I made was the same as if there hadn't been a redouble. We don't play lebensohl or any strange takeout calls. So why is my natural two notrump suddenly a confusing call?

I didn't want to hang partner by jumping to three notrump. After all, he was just balancing. Nor could I bid only three clubs when game prospects were in sight. So I made a simple standard invitational two-notrump bid.

I certainly didn't anticipate a disaster by making my natural, constructive bid. When I heard my partner's next call of three diamonds, I assumed he had a minimum takeout double with, perhaps, six diamonds and four hearts. If he had a strong hand, he would certainly have raised to game. So I made a disciplined pass of three diamonds. That ended the auction and there we were in a silly three-diamond contract, cold for two notrump. So I ask you, reader, you be the judge. Which was the confusing (and losing) call? Was it my two notrump (for +120) or his three diamonds (for -300)?

Matthew: Now just a minute. Let them hear me out before they judge. This was not your everyday situation. In fact, it was quite a tricky position.

You say that West's redouble did not change the meaning of your two-notrump call, but I think it did create doubt. We all agree that pass of the redouble would have been for penalties. Therefore, you were forced to make a bid. Suppose you held two four-card suits (for example: ♠ x x x ♡ K x ◇ J 10 x x ♣ Q x x x). You would surely prefer bidding 2NT for takeout rather than guessing which minor to bid at the three level.

West dealer   North (Pamela)

All vul
- ♠ Q 9 2
- ♡ 9 7 3
- ♢ 5 4 3
- ♣ A K Q 6

West

- ♠ A J 10 8 7 4
- ♡ A 8
- ♢ 6
- ♣ 10 9 8 7

East

- ♠ 6 3
- ♡ K Q J 5
- ♢ J 10 9 8 7
- ♣ 3 2

South (Matthew)

- ♠ K 5
- ♡ 10 6 4 2
- ♢ A K Q 2
- ♣ J 5 4

	Pamela		Matthew
West	North	East	South
2 ♠	pass	pass	double
redouble	2 NT	pass	3 ◊
(all pass)			

Now examine the evidence I was looking at: namely the ♠K doubleton. West surely had a strong spade suit for his redouble. So it was even more likely you had bid two notrump for takeout; otherwise, where was your spade stopper?

Finally, there's Dave Mason's theory: When in doubt, bid. Can you imagine the disaster of playing two notrump, vulnerable, down six, when all the time we are cold for three diamonds?

And finally, finally, why didn't you use the principle? Surely when I bid three diamonds, there had to be some doubt in your mind about my holding. First of all, why did three diamonds have to be a weak hand? Don't we play in most auctions that a double followed by a suit bid is strong? And second, couldn't you assume that I may have misinterpreted your two notrump and was bidding my better minor? Would it have been so terrible to rebid three notrump over three diamonds? So you go down one — what's the big deal? Sometimes you get lucky and make a close three notrump. Maybe East would have led the ♡K and done something stupid like continue hearts at trick two.*

Don't you have sympathy for a partner who bids when in doubt?

---

*If East continues with a low heart, he will be squeezed in the reds.

Pamela: Yes, I have sympathy, but what has that got to do with winning bridge? If being a good partner means giving up on playing the right contract, what's the point? Granted, your idea of playing two notrump for takeout has some merit. But I recommend discussing it with me before using it. A better maxim than "When in doubt, bid" may be "If we haven't discussed it, we don't play it."

Partnership Principles

· When partner makes a bid you don't understand:
(1) if it could be natural, assume it is; and
(2) if it could be forcing, assume it is.

Using this two-step rule, Matthew should have passed two notrump (1), and Pamela should have bid over three diamonds (2).

· The flip side is: Don't invent a new meaning for a bid at the table. Make a natural call and discuss your bright idea later.

· If you haven't discussed a convention or treatment, don't use it!

When we double and they redouble

When you make a takeout double and the next hand redoubles, when is partner's pass for penalty?

One general rule, which works quite well, is:
(1) Whenever they are in the contract of 1NT or higher, pass is for penalty.
(2) Below 1NT, whenever the passer is sitting over the *bidder* (the person who bid the suit that was doubled and redoubled), pass is for penalty.

Some examples:

1 ♢	double	redble	pass = not penalty ("under" the bidder)

1 ♠	pass	pass	double
redouble	pass = penalty ("over" the bidder)		

1 ♣	pass	1 ♠	double
redble	pass = not penalty ("under" the bidder)		

2 ♡	double	redble	pass = penalty (higher than 1♠ level)

Some pairs also play:

1 ♣	double	redble	pass = penalty

This is to prevent third hand from redoubling with short clubs. Choose your rules and stick to them.

Chapter 5: Two Styles — Aggressive and Conservative

Before we start our discussion, here are five bidding problems. Try them on for size:

1. Everybody vul: ♠ J 6 4 ♡ Q J 2 ◇ A K Q 3 2 ♣ 9 8
2. Everybody vul: ♠ K Q J 8 6 ♡ 10 9 5 4 ◇ 4 3 ♣ 9 7
3. Not vul vs. vul: ♠ J 7 ♡ A 10 6 5 3 ◇ 7 5 3 2 ♣ 6 3
4. Everybody vul: ♠ J 9 6 5 2 ♡ K 7 ◇ J 4 2 ♣ K J 2
5. Vul vs. not: ♠ 8 ♡ K 10 6 3 2 ◇ 2 ♣ Q J 9 6 5 4

All deals are at teams. On the first two, your RHO opens 1♡. Do you overcall or pass?

On the third, partner passes and RHO opens 1♣. Would you consider a 1♡ overcall?

On the fourth deal, RHO passes, you pass and LHO opens one heart in third chair. Partner passes and RHO bids two clubs, Drury. You pass and LHO bids two diamonds, showing a light opening bid. Partner passes and RHO signs off in two hearts. Would you bid two spades now?

On the fifth deal, LHO opens the bidding one spade. Partner passes and RHO bids 1NT. Do you overcall or pass? If you like, you have in your arsenal an overcall of three clubs to show clubs and hearts.

* * *

Matthew: There are two extremes in the world of interference bidding: those players who bid every chance they get and those who always have a good hand for their overcall (or raise). Is one method better than the other? I would say no, because there are various factors involved. I have prepared a simple chart:

Matthew's Overcall Chart

Busy Bidding works	Conservative Style works
• against weak opponents	• against strong opponents
• when not vul	• when vul
• with a conservative partner	• with an aggressive partner

From my chart, you can see when busy bidding works well and when a conservative style is the better strategy. Busy bidding fools weak opponents. You can talk them out of a game by overcalling and raising on light hands, but the same strategy often backfires against strong opponents, who will still bid game and now play the hand better with the information you've provided. On other occasions your overcall may help your strong opponents reach a better contract than they would have reached without the overcall.

It is safer to bid a lot when you are not vul, because if you go down, it's only 50 a trick. When you are vulnerable, obviously you have to be careful.

I was going to add here that at pairs it's safer to be a busy bidder than at team games, but I decided not to distinguish the two forms of scoring, because it can actually be more dangerous to bid at pairs, especially when minus 200 looms in the picture. Also, at pairs, you are more apt to get doubled at a low level than at teams.

Finally, the partnership element comes into play. If you are a busy bidder, it's to your advantage to be facing a conservative player, who will take your bids with a grain of salt. And every rubber bridge player will tell you that if you're facing an aggressive partner, you'd better watch your step before entering the bidding on dubious values.

Pamela: Your points are well spoken, but I would have to recommend the conservative style over the aggressive in general. The psychological stress on a busy-bidder's partner can be very high and often leads to the breakup of partnerships.

While the aggressive bidders are afraid of missing something, the conservative bidders get more plus scores and are less apt to have a disaster.

Matthew: Well, this depends on what you mean by disaster. If you mean going for 800, yes, conservative overcalls avoid this. But missing a vulnerable game may also be labeled "a disaster."

Pamela: True, but it's not the same type of disaster. When you miss a close game, it's usually a missed opportunity. When you go for 800, you can feel the blood dripping on the table. The latter is far more psychologically damaging and more likely to cause friction and muddled thinking on the following boards. I call these type of bidders: "busy bees." They are the type of players who bid every chance they get.

When a busy bee has a choice between passing and bidding, you'll always find him in there making lead-directing bids or trying to disrupt the opponents' auction. This sometimes works brilliantly but more often it destroys partnership trust, especially when the busy bee gets nailed.

One of the guidelines for passing in a close situation occurs when you have to make a two-level overcall in a minor suit to get into the auction. Notice I said minor suit. I like this rule: Over one spade on your right, overcall two hearts if it's close, because game in a major suit is possible. But a light overcall in a minor is fruitless. Many players would deem it perfectly normal to bid two diamonds on the South hand on the following page. But is it wise?

East dealer   North
All vul   ♠ A 7 5 3
              ♡ 10 9 8 4
              ◊ 9 5
              ♣ K 6 5

West (Pamela)   East (Matthew)
♠ Q 10 8 2   ♠ K 9
♡ 3   ♡ A K 7 6 5
◊ 10 8 7 6 4   ◊ J
♣ 10 4 3   ♣ A Q J 7 2

           South
           ♠ J 6 4
           ♡ Q J 2
           ◊ A K Q 3 2
           ♣ 9 8

West	North	East	South
—	—	1 ♡	2 ◊
pass	pass	double	(all pass)

I teach my students not to overcall at the two level in a minor suit without six cards in the trump suit. This may sound very strict but it is valid. Many writers today who expound on bridge have wrongly taught that when in doubt it is always better to bid than pass. This is simply not so.

On this hand from a team match South bid two diamonds and went down three doubled (he scored one spade and four trump tricks). If I were staring at an ace and a king plus a doubleton diamond (the North hand), and my partner overcalled two diamonds, I would be shocked to watch him go for 800. I would also find a new partner.

Matthew: Innocent. I am innocent of any wrong doing here, and not only that, I firmly agree with my wife. Our teammates on both this occasion, and another one where the overcaller had: ♠ K Q J 8 6 ♡ 10 9 5 4 ♢ 4 3 ♣ 9 7 and bid one spade over a one-heart opening, were Billy Eisenberg and Alan Sontag. It didn't occur to them to overcall on either hand, which is why they are world champions. (The one-spade overcall at our table also went for 800.) When another top player mentioned that he would over-call at matchpoints but not at teams, I suggested that he was right, minus 800 is a bad team score but a fine matchpoint result.

My sarcastic point was that even at matchpoints there is no safety (in fact, there's less safety) in overcalling light. Now I agree that lead-directing overcalls are important, but they must be weighed against the risk of a huge set. Granted, on the hand where South overcalled two diamonds, South got a little unlucky that we were able to nail him. But again, that is why my chart is so important to study. The overcalls of two diamonds and one spade had two strikes against them: the player who overcalled was vulnerable and he was playing against strong opponents.

Pamela: What's worse than a particularly bad result is the strain busy bidding puts on a partnership. It's difficult enough to tolerate lapses in judgment or card play errors without the additional burden of needless risk-taking. Aside from going for numbers, a busy overcall may direct your opponents to a better contract than is reachable if they were left to their own devices. Look at this deal from the Bermuda Bowl final of 1980, USA vs. Pakistan:

 Questions on overcalls

Does your partner overcall on four-card suits?

What does it mean if he fails to overcall the first time but later overcalls? (See page 154.)

What's the worst overcall you can expect?

Board 2   North
East dealer   ♠ K 8 2
N-S vul   ♡ J 4
                 ◇ A 9
                 ♣ K Q 9 8 5 4

West   East
♠ J 7   ♠ 10 9 5 4
♡ A 10 6 5 3   ♡ K Q 8
◇ 7 5 3 2   ◇ Q J 10 4
♣ 6 3   ♣ J 7

                 South
                 ♠ A Q 6 3
                 ♡ 9 7 2
                 ◇ K 8 6
                 ♣ A 10 2

CLOSED ROOM

West	North	East	South
Masood	Solodar	Zia	Arnold
—	—	pass	1 ♣
pass	2 ♣	pass	2 NT
pass	3 NT	(all pass)	

OPEN ROOM

West	North	East	South
Meckstroth	Munir	Rodwell	Fazli
—	—	pass	1 ♣
1 ♡	2 ♡	3 ♡	3 ♠
pass	4 ♣	pass	5 ♣
(all pass)			

In the Closed Room, Russ Arnold and John Solodar had a fairly natural auction to the normal three-notrump game. Perhaps Arnold (South) should have bid a stopper after the inverted raise by his partner, but one can hardly blame him for taking the practical approach with his 4-3-3-3 shape. West led a heart against three notrump, for a fast down one.

In the Open Room, Jeff Meckstroth overcalled one heart on the West cards. Jeff is undoubtedly one of the world's best players, but this time his light bidding backfired when his partner raised and North-South were alerted to the hole in the heart suit. They fled to the rare five-of-a-minor contract, where they rested successfully. Twelve imps went to Pakistan.

Matthew: Style is so important in partnership bridge. Perhaps this proves that very often a bid is not good or bad by itself, but only in the context of the players at the table. It was the style of Arnold-Solodar to bid to three notrump on balanced hands, not worrying about stoppers in suits unbid by the opponents — a very traditional style that was unsuccessful on this occasion. Likewise, it was the style of Meckstroth-Rodwell to overcall super-light at favorable vulnerability. This "live by the sword — die by the sword" style is often successful, but it wasn't here.

If you're playing in a partnership (or even if you are somewhat of a solo player, with many partners), it pays to adopt a style and stick to it. Then when things go wrong, you don't have to blame yourself or partner — the percentages will be with you if you succeed most of the time in your adopted style. In short: Don't choose someone else's style. Be yourself. Do what works for you.

Pamela: And when you play with me, Matthew, what works for you is normal overcalls and not bidding notrump without stoppers in all the suits.

Matthew: This is true, which is why we tend to succeed. But I'm not sure if it's our style that's successful or the fact that we both play the same style. There's no doubt that busy bees create a more dangerous atmosphere at the table and if you ask a busy bee how he can make such atrocious-looking bids, he'll tell you that even when he's wrong, he rarely gets caught. The following example is from the 1996 Vanderbilt final.

North dealer   North
E-W vul   ♠ K 3
                ♡ J 9 8
                ◇ A Q 9 8
                ♣ 10 6 5 4

West   East
♠ 10 8   ♠ J 9 6 5 2
♡ 6 5 4 2   ♡ K 7
◇ K 6 3   ◇ J 4 2
♣ A Q 8 7   ♣ K J 2

                South
                ♠ A Q 7 4
                ♡ A Q 10 3
                ◇ 10 7 5
                ♣ 9 3

West	North	East	South
Stansby	Hamman	Martel	Wolff
—	pass	pass	1 ♡
pass	2 ♣ (1)	pass	2 ◇ (2)
pass	2 ♡	2 ♠	double (3)
pass	3 ◇	(all pass)	

(1) Drury
(2) a light opening bid
(3) He meant it as penalty; his partner misread it.

Matthew: Look at that two-spade bid by Martel (East). He is vul against not at imps. Personally, I would never have the nerve to make such a bid. How can East compete for the partscore on such a rag at the risk of going for a number? Didn't we learn in the first book of team bridge that we do not bring back -800's to our teammates?

But look what happened. He caught partner with the absolute wrong hand, he got doubled, and he not only survived but he won imps! North pulled South's double and South misguessed the play in three diamonds, going down one. At the other table, North played in two diamonds, making two overtricks.

Pamela: Copying what the masters do is not always a bright idea. I think a lot depends on who you are. If you are Chip Martel, your opponents play safe and do not defend a vulnerable partscore. If you are a lesser mortal, your opponents defend and you go for 800 on the East cards.

Another point here is that players at all levels seem to have lost the ability to penalize the opponents. The word "double" has come to mean "let's compete" rather than "let's collect a juicy penalty."

Matthew: But this is not what I learned by those who taught me team bridge. One of my dad's favorite partners was "Chic" Robbins, who once asked me the following question: "Your partner opens the bidding one spade and you raise to two spades. The player on your left overcalls three clubs and your partner doubles. Are you more likely to pull this double at pairs or teams?"

"Teams," I answered, quickly and stupidly. "It's not safe to pass at teams, because if they make it, it's a game."

"Wrong. You are more likely to pull at Pairs, where partner may be doubling for a one- or two-trick set. At teams, you can be sure that partner has a strong trump stack, otherwise he would never risk doubling."

Pamela: Nevertheless, the world of bridge in the 1990's has changed regarding the double. Look at this example from the 1995 Bermuda Bowl final between the United States and Canada:

East dealer
E-W vul

North
♠ 6 4
♡ Q J 9
◇ K 10 8 5 3
♣ 10 8 2

West
♠ K Q J 9 5
♡ 7 4
◇ Q J 9 7 4
♣ 3

East
♠ 8
♡ K 10 6 3 2
◇ 2
♣ Q J 9 6 5 4

South
♠ A 10 7 3 2
♡ A 8 5
◇ A 6
♣ A K 7

OPEN ROOM

West Baran	North Wolff	East Molson	South Hamman
—	—	pass	1 ♣ (17+)
1 NT	double	pass	pass
2 ◇	pass	pass	2 NT
pass	3 NT	(all pass)	

CLOSED ROOM

West Rodwell	North Mittelman	East Meckstroth	South Gitelman
—	—	pass	1 ♠
pass	1 NT	3 ♣ (C+H)	double
3 ♡	4 ◇	pass	5 ◇
double	(all pass)		

Pamela: In the Open Room, West's one-notrump overcall of South's big club showed a two-suiter, spades and diamonds or hearts and clubs. It appeared that West would go for a huge number in two diamonds doubled, but he escaped.

Matthew: Perhaps North thought that he and his partner were playing the double of two diamonds as takeout and South thought they were playing the double as penalty, so he couldn't double either.

Pamela: I think one reason why overly-aggressive partnerships get away with "bad" overcalls is that partnerships play too many ambiguous doubles. When I played rubber bridge back at the Mayfair Club in New York, you couldn't possibly escape the ax when you hit a misfit — and vulnerable no less! The lesson here is easy: Take the "competitive double" and junk it. Once both hands show values, all doubles must be played as penalty.

Now look at the second auction. Though I have some sympathy for East's two-suited overcall of three clubs, it was the wrong day for him — or at least should have been. As you say, North-South must have been playing the double of three clubs as takeout, though I think North should have realized partner had to hold clubs when West took a preference to three hearts.

Matthew: This is the busy bees' argument. Even when they get caught, they escape! Can you imagine if I had bid three clubs as your partner? It would go double, three hearts by you, double, all pass, and I would have to leave the room rather than risk facing you as I put down the dummy.

Pamela: I would never say a word, darling. I would play the hand, go down 1400 or so, and then leave the room myself.

Partnership Principles

There are some successful partnerships that exist nicely

with both players bidding their heads off. They get a lot of publicity, especially when they reach a lucky slam or doubled game that makes. And they can make life miserable for their opponents at times. But they have some horrible results, too, which we rarely see in print.

These partnerships can live with an occasional disaster probably because they never socialize with each other away from the table. But most husband-wife partnerships cannot withstand such disasters and many partnerships made up of two friends also have trouble coping with disasters. For these partnerships we suggest:

• Don't overcall in a five-card minor at the two-level, unless you hold a very strong hand.

• Don't make ultra-light, lead-directing overcalls at the one level.

• Don't raise partner in competition if you are going to be sick when he sacrifices over a game bid on your left.

• When you make a risky vulnerable bid, make sure you're the one who will play the hand if it gets doubled.

• Choose a style, aggressive or conservative, but make sure you and your partner play the *same* style, so there will be no recriminations when the occasional disaster strikes. When a busy bee partners a conservative, someone must adjust (usually the conservative must take a stiff drink and put on his busy-bee hat, because otherwise the conservative will feel left out of the action).

• Once you and your partner have made a free bid (i.e., not a forced bid), all doubles should be for penalty.

Chapter 6: Threading the Needle

Pamela: My husband and I are blessed in our marriage, because we love to do things together. But when we play bridge we don't often face each other at the table. This is because playing bridge with your spouse is a dangerous sport. During our long years of marriage, we've gone through periods of partnership harmony and partnership misery at the table.

It's easy to understand why a husband and wife can have problems as a bridge partnership. Emotions get in the way. Expecting him to play perfectly, I take it as a personal insult if he makes a mistake. Also, we have different philosophies on how the game should be played. Matthew likes to "thread the needle" (i.e., do whatever is necessary to achieve the perfect result on each hand). This might involve, for example, passing a forcing bid or suddenly making up a new meaning for a double. He likes to invent new bids and carding methods at the end of each session to perfect any hands that went astray. I prefer "practical bridge." I set no traps for partner and never worry about my methods as long as they work most of the time.

Sometimes a marriage-partnership needs a rest. This rest period can last as long as a year or two, then suddenly, without knowing why, it changes; you are suddenly very compatible and understand each other perfectly. After a brief spell of bliss, however, it can turn overnight into "I never want to see his/her face at the table again." When this happens, you can still enjoy bridge together if it's a team game. He gets a partner, she gets a partner, and you play as a team.

This deal is from such a period in our lives. It comes from the New York Cavendish Swiss Teams, an annual team game with cash prizes. (In 1997 it was moved to Las Vegas.)

On this particular occasion, we played as a five-person team with Jimmy Cayne, Michael Rosenberg and Zia Mahmood. We were all friends and we all knew one another's style, which allowed each of us to have two or three partnerships. I played with everybody on the team except Matthew, and we never lost a match. Granted, it was a pretty strong group, but the secret to our success was not just talent. We had a simple bidding system and no complicated understandings. We knew each other's style and catered to it. Thus, when I played with Michael, who likes delicate bidding, I tried to bid delicately. When I played with Zia, who likes to throw knuckle balls at his opponents, I put on an extra big catcher's mitt and took his bids and plays with a grain of salt. When I played with Jimmy, who is a tough rubber bridge player and likes to keep things practical, I also was practical. This hand is a good example. But I will give it to you from my partner's point of view, because he was faced with this difficult bidding decision:

♠ A 3 2   ♡ 10 6 4 3   ◇ K Q J   ♣ A J 6

Everyone was vulnerable and Jimmy heard me open the bidding in first seat with two diamonds. This was straightforward, a weak two-bid in diamonds. Jimmy's RHO, a strong player, overcalled two hearts and Jimmy had his first decision to make. He could see right away that I had a good weak two-bid. Why? Because he was staring at the king, queen, jack of diamonds! This is a favorite principle of strong money-bridge players: When you are surprised (shocked in some cases) by your partner's bid, because you hold cards that he should hold, you should sit up in your seat and realize that partner must hold a great hand. If I was opening a weak two-bid in diamonds, vulnerable, without three honors, I must hold strong compensating values and distribution.

Thus, Jimmy knew we had at least nine winners and probably more, but he couldn't be sure whether the final contract should be three notrump or five diamonds. It depended on my heart holding. So he cuebid three hearts. This direct cuebid asked me to bid three notrump with a heart stopper. And this is what I did. But now Jimmy's RHO surprised us all by bidding four hearts. The auction:

Pamela		Jimmy	
South	West	North	East
2 ◇	2 ♡	3 ♡	pass
3 NT	4 ♡	?	

Jimmy's choices were:
(1) pass, (2) double, (3) four notrump, and (4) five diamonds. What would you call? Decide before reading on.

Jimmy's thoughts were something like this. Pass, if it is forcing and says, "I don't know what to do, help me, please," is the perfect call on paper. But from a practical viewpoint, it is quite dangerous. It appears that we've bid a vulnerable game and that the opponent is sacrificing, but on the other hand, the player who bid four hearts is also vulnerable, and he's quite a strong player. We started with a weak two-bid, and partner may think that after a weak two-bid start, forcing passes don't apply. In any case, there is a good deal of room for error when partner may have already stretched to open with a weak two-bid (she certainly is not going to fancy bidding again with the weak diamond suit she holds), and she may decide to pass it out. No, pass may be perfect bridge but it's a bad partnership call.

Double feels like the obvious choice. They're vulnerable, partner must have the ◇A and a heart honor and something else. Why not take the sure plus? But what about RHO's bidding. It is awfully suspicious. For him to overcall two hearts and later bid four hearts on his own, a sequence begging to be doubled, he must have a surprise or two in store for us. A void in diamonds is very likely and a strong side suit perhaps?

Four notrump is possible. Come to think of it, partner was about to declare a cold nine-trick three notrump (six diamonds, two aces and a heart). We're only one trick short of 10, and maybe partner has an extra king, or a seventh diamond in view of her weak suit.

Five diamonds seems like too much. There's no ruffing value in the hand, and the same number of tricks appears to be likely in either notrump or diamonds. No, the best call, the most practical call, is four notrump.

This is what Jimmy bid and the full layout was:

South dealer	North (Jimmy)
All vul	♠ A 3 2
	♡ 10 6 4 3
	◇ K Q J
	♣ A J 6

West	East
♠ K 10 4	♠ Q J 9 8 7
♡ K Q J 9 8 7 5	♡ 2
◇ —	◇ 8 7 2
♣ 9 8 3	♣ K Q 10 7

South (Pamela)
♠ 6 5
♡ A
◇ A 10 9 6 5 4 3
♣ 5 4 2

Pamela		Jimmy	
South	West	North	East
2 ◇	2 ♡	3 ♡	pass
3 NT	4 ♡	4 NT	(all pass)

Pamela: I had that extra trick he was counting on. If he had passed it around to me, I don't know what I would have done, and I was real glad he didn't.

Notice that I had a difficult choice of calls as dealer. I chose to open a weak two diamonds, but I could have opened three diamonds or passed. I decided against three diamonds because of the two defensive tricks and I don't like to fool my partner. But even though I had a seventh diamond, I opened two diamonds, believing it was more practical to describe a hand with length in diamonds than not to bid at all. Also, I like to take advantage of being dealer and get my suit in before the bidding gets too high.

At the other table, a former world champion in my seat "threaded the needle" by passing the South hand:

	Zia		Michael
South	West	North	East
pass	4 ♡	pass	pass
5 ◊	pass	6 ◊	double
(all pass)			

Six diamonds went down two. My husband was sitting out this round, and I did not scold him for any errors.

Matthew: (Aside: Very funny.) I happen to agree with your two-diamond opening. But don't you think part of your success on this hand came from your partner "threading the needle"? Take a look at his four-notrump bid again. He could count only nine sure tricks: six diamonds, your heart stopper, and two aces. Most practical players would double four hearts, take the money and run. But Jimmy used his imagination in picturing a diamond void in West's hand (I think it's amazing that four hearts was laydown!), and then "sacrificed" in four notrump.

I'm all for practical bridge and avoiding disaster, but sometimes the difference between a good bid and a great bid is the

South dealer North (Jimmy)
All vul

♠ A 3 2
♡ 10 6 4 3
◇ K Q J
♣ A J 6

West   East
♠ K 10 4   ♠ Q J 9 8 7
♡ K Q J 9 8 7 5 ♡ 2
◇ —   ◇ 8 7 2
♣ 9 8 3   ♣ K Q 10 7

South (Pamela)
♠ 6 5
♡ A
◇ A 10 9 6 5 4 3
♣ 5 4 2

Pamela		Jimmy	
South	West	North	East
2 ◇	2 ♡	3 ♡	pass
3 NT	4 ♡	4 NT	(all pass)

difference between losing and winning. The best tennis players go for the sidelines, not the center of the court. And on this deal, your partner smashed the ball directly on the white chalk.

Pamela: You may discuss your sideline smashes with your tennis cronies. Jimmy's four notrump was as practical as Jacqui Mitchell's apple pie. He didn't know whether the opponents could make a game, so he simply took out insurance with what could be at worst a one-trick set. The point here is that he kept the ball in play, not that he went for the sidelines. And when you keep the ball in play, sometimes you happen to hit a winner.

Matthew: OK, OK. Forgive me for suggesting your result was sensational rather than ordinary.

Partnership Principles

• Don't put pressure on your partner by making a "forcing" pass in a situation where it isn't absolutely clear your pass is forcing. The perfect bid in theory is often dangerous at the table, *when it requires that partner read it.*

• When you have a choice between passing or making a number

of bids that don't fit your hand exactly, choose the bid that is closest to describing your hand.

• When you have a long, strong suit and a void, such as the West hand in our last deal, don't fool around with a simple overcall — go directly to game. If West had jumped to four hearts over the two-diamond opening, North-South would have needed to be Houdinis to land in four notrump.

• Watch out for players who overcall at a low level and later bid game by themselves. There's a good chance they were "walking the dog," trying to buy the hand or get doubled.

 Cuebid confusion

When does a cuebid at the three level ask for a stopper and when does it show one?

This is easy! Follow the the "one-two rule."

(1) The cuebid asks for a stopper when only one suit has been bid by the opponents.

(2) The cuebid shows a stopper if two suits have been bid by the opponents.

Example:

West	North	East	South
1 ♣	1 ♦	double	2 ♦

3 ♦ = asks for stopper

But if South had bid 2♡ or 2♠, West would be showing a diamond stopper.

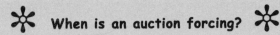

When is an auction forcing?

Don't forget to discuss this difficult topic. Some clear rules can alleviate the stress. Most tournament partnerships play something like this:

• Pass is forcing at the three level when one of you has at least invited game.

• At the four level or higher, pass is forcing when one of you has invited or bid game, and one of you has (a) cuebid, or (b) made a two-over-one, limit jump raise or any strong response, or (c) bid two suits.

Example:

West	North	East	South
1 ♠	2 ♡	2 ♠	3 ♡
4 ♠	5 ♡	pass	

Pass is not forcing. But if opener had bid 4♣, 4♢ or 4♡, *pass* would be forcing.

Note: Some pairs play that pass is forcing at the four level or higher whenever your side bids a game vulnerable against not. This rule has its ups and downs. Each partnership must decide.

• The meaning of a forcing pass is usually: "I'm not sure whether to double or bid." But there's more to it. Many pairs play that pass could be the start of a slam try if you bid on the subsequent round. See pages 132-134 for more on this topic.

Chapter 7: Experiments

Matthew: The first hand of any event is always the most difficult for me. My mind isn't working yet, and sometimes I'm nervous. I'm not ready for a bidding problem, and I often overlook something in the cardplay. In physical sports, players warm up, volley, and do exercises. Before a bridge session, why don't we do the same?

The following deal was played in a four-session Mixed Pairs, but for my wife and me it lasted two. Like most of the competitors, we did not warm up beforehand. Needless to say the very first board presented a problem.

First seat, not vul versus vul, I picked up:

♠ 5 3   ♡ J 4 3   ◇ K Q 10 8 2   ♣ 10 8 4

I passed and my LHO opened one spade. Pamela passed, and RHO bid two notrump, alerted as Jacoby Two Notrump, a game force with a spade fit. At this point I was sorry I hadn't opened an "indecent" weak two-bid in diamonds, just to get the lead. Then I realized that we were at favorable vulnerability and that I was unlikely to be doubled at the three level when they had a known vulnerable game. By bidding three diamonds, I could get my partner off to the killing lead and start the session with a bang.

What did not occur to me was the fact that the vulnerability was tempting for a sacrifice, and an overcall might lead partner into an error if she had a diamond fit and decided to take the sacrifice in five diamonds. Yet even if I had thought of this, the lead-directing bid is extremely tempting. What would you do? Pass or bid?

I didn't even hesitate. I saw an opportunity to take advantage of the opponents' convention, the vulnerability, and my passed-hand status all in one fell swoop. Well, the next three bids I heard were: four spades, five diamonds (uh oh), double! The opening lead was made and this was the layout:

South dealer	North (Pamela)	
E-W vul	♠ 7 2	
	♡ Q 7 6	
	◇ J 7 4 3	
	♣ A 6 5 3	

West		East
♠ A K 10 6 4		♠ Q J 9 8
♡ K 8 2		♡ A 10 9 5
◇ A 5		◇ 9 6
♣ 9 7 2		♣ K Q J

	South (Matthew)	
	♠ 5 3	
	♡ J 4 3	
	◇ K Q 10 8 2	
	♣ 10 8 4	

Matthew		Pamela	
South	West	North	East
pass	1 ♠	pass	2 NT
3 ◇	4 ♠	5 ◇	double
(all pass)			

I went down a quick 900. In those days the scoring of doubled nonvul undertricks was 100, 300, 500, 700, 900. Then I made the mistake of explaining the sound reasoning of my bid.

Pamela: Don't explain. If you want to make creative bids, do it with someone else. When you slip in a favorable overcall higher than the one level, you should be looking for a sacrifice. I thought you had some shape, maybe 5-5 in the minors or diamonds and hearts; otherwise why hadn't you opened a diamond preempt?

Matthew: Ah, you see, that's just my point. I thought that my being a passed hand would deny the distribution for a sacrifice. Now you have to admit it was right to lead a diamond. A heart lead is disastrous, and a trump lead gives them time to set up a pitch. Overtricks are important at matchpoints, and holding four spades to 10 tricks would have been a good score.

Pamela: My husband and I already play a uniform system of opening leads. Against major-suit games, without any clear clues from the bidding, we try to lead in order of preference: an ace-king, a singleton, a king-queen, a queen-jack, or a jack-ten. Barring touching honors, we try to make a safe lead — one that is least likely to give away a trick. So we almost never start with an unsupported ace, or lead from a suit headed by a king or queen. We prefer to lead from nothing, or, as a last resort, a trump (a trump can be dangerous, because it may pick up partner's honor). In this case, my choice against four spades would have been between a trump and a diamond. With three trumps, I would lead a trump, knowing my partner had only one and it couldn't hurt. But with two trumps, I would have led a diamond. A diamond lead is not absolutely safe by a long shot, but it is the safest lead with this hand.

As the reader can guess by now, the point of telling you all this is not only to recommend a solid, partnership system of opening leads, but also to prove that my husband's brilliant lead-director wasn't necessary.

Partnership Principles

• Don't experiment at the table. When you think about doing something new and exciting, stop yourself! Check later to see if the experiment would have worked. If so, discuss it with your partner and see if partner would have been annoyed by the action or will agree to play it that particular way in the future.

• If you have a regular partnership, think about adopting a set of rules for opening leads. It helps to know partner's tendencies. We recommend conservative leads, in general. However, if your partner likes to lead aggressively, you will need to make more lead-directing bids to steer him away from his strength-leads, and he should know that.

• Do your warm-ups. If it's not practical to play a few deals before an event, read about a few deals in a bridge book. For the bidding, we recommend Terence Reese's "Develop Your Bidding Judgment." For the play of the cards, the best is "Squeezes" by Love. One page of this book will get your mind counting and working. And like an athlete, you will be tuned up for Board #1.

❋   *Opening-lead styles*   **❋**

It's important to have a knowledge of your partner's style. In the bidding, it's easy to distinguish an aggressive player from a conservative one. But on opening lead, it can be useful, too. Does your partner like to lead from honors or is he stingy?

    A J x x   A J x x

x   Q 9 x   x   K 10 x

In both cases partner leads low. If you know your partner's tendencies, it will help you to judge the position and your best play.

Chapter 8: Inhibitions

Matthew: I'm not a down-the-middle player. I admit this freely. But I'm not what you'd call a wild player either. I like to think of myself as creative. But if I had my choice of partners, I'd pick the opposite: a steady-Eddie type who always has his bids and never makes unusual leads.

Now this may sound crazy, but perhaps being one of these extremes is better than being in the middle. At least, it's better in the sense that your partner knows what to expect of you. For example, with a creative type, you know you have to watch out for the underlead of an ace on opening lead or the lead of the queen from queen-third. And you are always alert to the possibility. Whereas facing a steady Eddie, you know it's easy to pass when he makes a penalty double and you know when he leads the fourth-best deuce, he's got four of them.

But I'm the type of player who likes to throw a curve ball now and then by making a daring lead or risky double, or, even stranger, by trapping on the first round of bidding and then entering later. And my partner doesn't know when it's coming. But then neither do the opponents. Nevertheless, I admit my type must be the most difficult to partner.

Pamela: Well, you've taken my breath away. So why do you do it? Why not stick to one style (the steady-Eddie style, please)? Why are you one day straight out of the book and the next day a mad scientist? Can't we just win when the opponents make more mistakes than we do? Wouldn't that be fun?

Matthew: It's fun to win, I suppose, no matter what our style, but I love the game too much to just sit there like a robot and never take any chances. Unfortunately, this has gotten me into trouble on more than one occasion. Even under normal circumstances, I have to watch my step playing with you, darling. But remember the time you were seven-months pregnant with our first child and we were playing in Reykjavik, Iceland?

Those days I really had to watch my step, since the last thing I wanted to do was upset the pregnancy. (Boy, was my style cramped!)

Pamela: Cramped? On the first board of the team event, the opponents climbed slowly to three notrump, and you made one of your speculative doubles. Lucky for you, the opponents ran to four of a minor even though three notrump was cold.

Matthew: This fetched no disapproving comments from across the table, and no icy glares either.

Pamela: When your bravado works, I'm happy. Too bad it works so rarely.

Matthew: Well, I decided I had shot my wad, and for the rest of the event I held back and played a disciplined game. But near the very end I had the opportunity to make a brilliant play and I wasn't sure if I should do it or not. Let the readers decide:

North
♠ Q J 9
♡ K Q J 8 6 5
♢ A 6 2
♣ Q

West (You)
♠ K
♡ 10 7 3
♢ K J 10 8 5 4
♣ 9 8 6

West	North	East	South
—	1 ♡	pass	1 ♠
pass	2 ♠	pass	3 ♠
pass	4 ♠	(all pass)	

Suppose you lead a club against four spades. Partner wins the ace and returns the ♢7. Declarer now places his cards on the table and begins to think. You can now rule out his holding queen doubleton, or he would have put up the queen without a thought. So he holds three diamonds and is thinking whether to play the 9 or the queen. Is there anything you should be thinking about?

To start, let's picture declarer's highcards. He holds the ♣K, ♢Q and, therefore, only one ace. Partner has the ♠A or ♡A, probably the ♡A. Now follow some chess thinking. Suppose he plays the ♢Q. You cover. What will happen? He'll win in dummy and, desperate to pitch one or two of those diamonds away on club honors, he'll lead a trump to the ace, eschewing the finesse. Lovely. Your king will fall under the ace and he will have no more problems.

Can you do something about this? Well, suppose you don't cover the ♢Q. What a thought! He will now feel quite safe about the diamond situation. Probably he'll knock out the ♡A, planning to finesse the ♠Q to your king. Then you will triumphantly give partner a diamond ruff to set the contract!

Well, here's a chance to make the play of your bridge career. Will you do it? Here we go. Declarer has picked up his hand from the table and dislodged a card. It's the ◇Q. Quickly, do you cover or play low? (If you peeked already, it's OK.)

North dealer
E-W vul

North
♠ Q J 9
♡ K Q J 8 6 5
◇ A 6 2
♣ Q

West (Matthew)
♠ K
♡ 10 7 3
◇ K J 10 8 5 4
♣ 9 8 6

East (Pamela)
♠ 7 4 3 2
♡ A 9 4
◇ 7
♣ A 10 7 3 2

South
♠ A 10 8 6 5
♡ 2
◇ Q 9 3
♣ K J 5 4

West	North	East	South
—	1 ♡	pass	1 ♠
pass	2 ♠	pass	3 ♠
pass	4 ♠	(all pass)	

Matthew: At the table, I made the error of thinking: What if I'm wrong? What if somehow my brilliant play backfires? Will my wife go into premature labor? Will she ever speak to me again? Does it make sense to be a hero when it can only upset your pregnant partner?

When declarer finally played the ◇Q, I covered like a coward. Soon after my worst bridge fears were realized when he led a spade to the ace and made his contract.

Pamela: It's a sweet story, and if I were 20 years younger, I suppose I would buy it. But when have I ever inhibited your attempts at brilliancy? In fact, it was your brilliant plays that attracted me to you in the first place. (Aside: It certainly wasn't his money.) And as you said, Matthew, why be a hero when solid bridge will almost always win?

Matthew: When did I say that?

Pamela: On our first date.

Note: On the first date, solid bridge does win. After the wedding, it takes a little extra.

Pamela: Even though we lost points on this hand, we blitzed the match. It wasn't necessary to be brilliant. True, you might have won the Bols brilliancy prize, been applauded by cheering kibitzers, and been written up in newspapers all over the world. But is this enough to risk upsetting the solid foundations of a partnership?

Matthew: Very funny. The fact remains I was inhibited from the best part of my game: imaginative card play. One of the first strong players I ever partnered, Kyle Larsen, said to me before we sat down at the table: "Don't let me cramp your style." That's what I would like to hear when I play with you, too.

Pamela: Kyle Larsen played with you once. If he played with you more often, perhaps he would have asked you to do a little cramping. Sure, go ahead at the rubber bridge table and do whatever comes into your head. But brilliant plays do not win bridge tournaments.

Matthew: Well, they don't exactly hurt.

Pamela: Look, I won't chastise you for attempting brilliancies as long as they don't involve me. But if you're just as sensitive to me when I'm not pregnant — and to your male partners for that matter — you're apt to win a lot more championships.

Matthew: Could it be that it's boring to win? (Or am I getting too philosophical?) Anyway, if we were scoring this one, we would score it:

Covering with the ◇K = 0

Playing low on the ◇Q = 10 plus the Bols Brilliancy Prize

Partnership Principles

• Be a steady Eddie in the bidding and save your creativity for the cardplay.

• Don't blame your partner for your failure to find a brilliant defense.

• Don't play with pregnant partners unless you are prepared to cramp your style.

 Bridge and babies

Don't discuss bridge with your spouse while:

(1) baby is learning to crawl
(2) you are boiling baby's bottle
(3) baby is eating spaghetti

Chapter 9: Words of Encouragement

Matthew: You pick up, as East, the following hand in a Swiss Team match:

♠ 10 6 3 ♡ Q ◇ 10 9 8 7 5 2 ♣ 10 7 6

Your partner opens the bidding one heart and the next hand passes. Your first decision is whether to keep the bidding open or whether to pass. Checking the vulnerability, you see that you are not vulnerable and the opponents are vulnerable. The green light! Obviously at any other vulnerability you would not bid, but at favorable, you have a greater degree of safety and a greater reward for keeping the opponents out of game. In your arsenal of bids, you happen to be playing a jump shift as preemptive. Thus, you have the option of jumping to three diamonds. What is your choice, pass, one notrump, or three diamonds?

My first thought was that one notrump was out, because it would only lead partner astray. The idea of bidding three diamonds was a good one, but then I realized that partner may play me for a slightly better holding. If I caught her with a good hand and a diamond honor or two, she may rebid three notrump, whereupon I would hate to put down this dummy — what a disappointment!

So I decided to remain disciplined (for once) and I passed. I did hold a queen and a lot of high spotcards, and we play sound opening bids, so the odds of the opponents making a game were low. We had a minimum of 14 or 15 points between us. If partner held only a jack or queen more than minimum, they would hold less than the 25 points usually needed to bid a game.

The bidding proceeded: ·

Pamela		Matthew	
West	North	East	South
1 ♡	pass	pass	1 NT
pass	2 NT	pass	3 NT
(all pass)			

Ugh. They did bid the game! If only I could take back my first pass. Well, it's not over yet. After all, my partner and I play a very careful system of opening leads and we are quite capable on defense. If partner leads her fourth-best heart, it won't hurt, because I have the queen.

After some careful thought, my partner's lead hits the table face down. No questions, I say. Over it turns. Hmm, the ♡A. This could be good or bad. . . .

```
                      North
                      ♠ Q 8 7 4
                      ♡ J 10 6 2
                      ◇ A 6
                      ♣ K 9 2
                                        East (Matthew)
                                        ♠ 10 6 3
                                        ♡ Q
           ♡A         ┌─────┐           ◇ 10 9 8 7 5 2
                      │     │           ♣ 10 7 6
                      └─────┘
```

Not good. Not good at all. Look at those hearts in dummy. Oy vey, what a lead. Nevertheless, I steel myself to play the ♡Q in the most polite manner possible, and my face is kept as straight as can be. (Perhaps I should apologize — no, that's going too far.)

Partner continues with a low heart. Declarer wins in hand with the 8, plays the ♣A, a club to the king, and a third club to my partner's queen. She continues the heart attack with the king and a heart. But declarer wins in dummy, leads a spade to the ace, cashes the 13th club, then plays a diamond to the ace. On this trick, my partner's singleton queen falls, so declarer spreads her hand. She has one spade, two hearts, three diamonds and three clubs for a total of nine tricks. The full deal was:

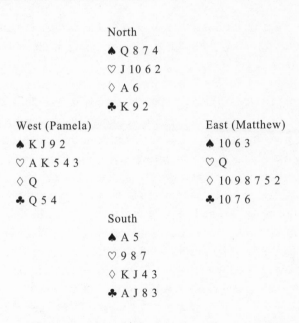

North
♠ Q 8 7 4
♡ J 10 6 2
◇ A 6
♣ K 9 2

West (Pamela)
♠ K J 9 2
♡ A K 5 4 3
◇ Q
♣ Q 5 4

East (Matthew)
♠ 10 6 3
♡ Q
◇ 10 9 8 7 5 2
♣ 10 7 6

South
♠ A 5
♡ 9 8 7
◇ K J 4 3
♣ A J 8 3

At this point, I grit my teeth (ever so gently), and slip my cards into the board without any sign of emotion. As the opponents begin to congratulate each other on their fine bidding (remember, declarer bid one notrump without a stopper and dummy made a light raise to two notrump — it was a 23-point game, after all), my wife looks me straight in the eye and says, her face slightly crimson, "How could you!"

At this point, I have a number of options, which I will share with you. Put yourself in my chair; what would you do? Choose one:

(1) Say you were sorry that you had not jump-shifted to three diamonds.

(2) Say you were sorry that you did not revoke in hearts.

(3) Pretend to be innocent and say that you do not know why she is upset, as you have done nothing unusual to provoke such an emotion.

(4) Look partner in the eye and say you would have made the same awful lead, possibly leaving out the word, "awful."

To score a ten on this problem, you had to answer — get ready — number (4), but you had to do it before you put the cards back in the board.

Pamela: Bridge is the only sport where partners and teammates think nothing of criticizing each other even in the heat of battle. Imagine my surprise when this incident occurred and afterwards, when I gave the hand to a (true) friend as an opening-lead problem, he said instantly upon seeing the four hands: "The contract was always cold no matter what you led." He went on to point out that after a low heart lead and a spade switch, if I cash the hearts and lead a fourth one, three rounds of diamonds by declarer will squeeze me. And if I continue spades, declarer can still make the contract by taking the backward finesse in clubs, leading the ♣J, picking up my queen and four club tricks in the process.

But no, this is not what my partner said at the table. My "supportive" partner just sat there, letting the pain of the situation sink deeper and deeper into my heart. I mean, when you have nothing good to say about something, you keep your mouth shut, right?

Matthew: I feel like Hamlet's uncle or something here. How deep did that silent dagger go? I mean it was very nice of your friend to give you that quick double-dummy analysis, but it was a bit much, wasn't it? I could easily hold the ♣Q third along with my heart honor and pass your one-heart opening. You want me to pamper you after a disaster? You want me to analyze every hand to show you where your mistakes didn't cost if we were playing against Belladonna?

Pamela: No, I want you to be a sympathetic partner. You know that I am trying my best on every deal and you should realize how bad I felt about my lead. Don't sit there stewing about it, like you did, but offer partner some words of encouragement, in the same way ball players pat the back of their teammates when a ball has been dropped or the pitcher has given up a home run.

My opening lead could have been right. You might have held, for example, a singleton small heart and good clubs or spades and I find the right switch at trick two. Who knows? The point is my lead was not abnormal and it might have been a low heart that cost the contract. Thus, you should immediately relieve my mental anguish by saying something nice, like "It will be the same result at the other table," or "I'm glad I wasn't on lead, or I would have been the one to lead the ♡A."

Matthew: Well, maybe, just maybe, you should have said something first. For example, you might have said, "Sorry, bad lead." That would have elicited a nice comeback from me.

Pamela: But don't you get it? It wasn't a bad lead. Why should I apologize for a normal lead that backfires? You're the one who should apologize, because you were the one who could have preempted to three diamonds and kept them out of game.

Matthew: (I had a feeling we would return to that.) When I first started out in this crazy game, I used to play bridge with my brother. Brothers have a hard time apologizing to each other, so we made a pact one day: We would apologize if we thought partner made an error. This system soon became obsolete when we went on an apology binge in the middle of the first session.

OK, perhaps I should have given you a pat on the back, but I think it's not an easy thing to do, human nature being what it is, especially when you drop my singleton queen, my one asset on defense. Even the great partnerships have a difficult time with this. Eddie Kantar once told me about the time his friend, Marshall Miles, was playing against Edgar Kaplan and Norman Kay, two of the kindest and most sympathetic partners in the business, and Marshall was having a great game to Kaplan and Kay's disappointment. Edgar was obviously perturbed by his terrible game. Then Norman goes for 800 on two hands in a row.

"Edgar," says Norman, "I am not trying to throw you."

Edgar says, "What do you want me to do, celebrate?"

Partnership Principles

• When your partner makes what appears to be a boner (whether it was a mistake or simply an unlucky bid or play), be aware that a supportive remark may help.

• The simplest remark in such a case is: "I would have done the same thing."

• It goes without saying (but we'll say it): Never, ever, make a face or sarcastic remark to partner at the table. And no matter how angry you get, never use a curse word.

• Another way to break the ice when things go wrong is to offer to get partner a cup of coffee.

• When it's close at favorable vulnerability between preempting or not, make the preempt. Partner should also be aware that the "green light is on."

Sticks and stones

Matthew: I was once playing against a married couple who were as kind and polite as could be. Suddenly, she put the dummy down and it wasn't what he wanted. He blurted out, "What the ---- are you doing . . . *Sweetheart?"* The lilt of "sweetheart" softened the verbal blow somewhat, but not enough.

Pamela: Some say it is healthy to let the anger out immediately. I knew someone who used to write in his private convention card nasty names about his partner ("board 6, idiot; board 7, birdbrain, etc."), but always kept a smile on his face. Unfortunately, once between rounds he left his card on the table when he went to the bathroom, and his partner opened it to copy a score.

> **Note:** We all know the saying: "Sticks and stones will break my bones but names will never hurt me." In bridge (and in life) this saying is wrong. We wouldn't recommend using a stick or a stone, but a physical blow eventually heals. A bad word, however, can remain in our memory forever.

Matthew: Fourteen years ago my wife said to me at the end of the session: "I played pretty well, didn't I?" I answered, "Well, you didn't have much to do." For 14 years that remark has come back to me in times of trouble. My advice is: Don't ever blurt out anything at the bridge table. It's a dangerous arena.

Pamela: P.S. Players who "don't have much to do" often find creative ways to lose points.

Part II

On Forming a Partnership

by Larry Cohen

Chapter 10: Love Thy Partner

It's been said that one's bridge partner can be as important as a marital partner. This saying might not score many points on Valentine's Day, but it will win masterpoints at the bridge table.

Learning how to handle the relationship with your bridge partner will do more for your results than reading any technical book on the game. I don't care if you know the name for every squeeze, and every form of Roman Keycard Blackwood — if your partnership is no good, you are at a big disadvantage.

If I were to name the top partnerships of the last decade, my list would be headed by Jeff Meckstroth-Eric Rodwell and Bob Hamman-Bobby Wolff. Sure, you say, those are brilliant players — no wonder they are on top of the list. But they are great partners. Hamman-Wolff play a fairly uncomplicated big-club system, and Meckwell play an 800-page highly artificial big-club system. The one connecting link is the way they are "partnerships" in every sense of the word.

When they get a bad result (and it happens more than you would think) there is no acrimony. It's always "on to the next board." There are no raised eyebrows, no "why didn't you do this," and absolutely no yelling, ranting, or ravings. The time to discuss these things is always after the session.

We'll come back to this later, but for now let's look at what goes into the formation of a bridge partnership.

My First Partner

Most of us want a partner who plays as well or better than we do.

That's the best way to achieve good results, as well as to learn. I was lucky enough to be in this situation at the start of my bridge career. When I first started playing duplicate, at the age of 14, a lot of the people at the club were helpful. Father Robert M. Panek was a very experienced player without a regular partner. He saw that I had potential, and he graciously formed a partnership with me. He was by far the better player, and I learned plenty.

Not only did he teach me conventions, but he taught me deportment at the table. The first few times I played with him I was on my best behavior, but, as often happens when you get familiar and comfortable with someone, bad traits soon came out. One evening at the local duplicate I put down the dummy and watched him lose a few unnecessary tricks in the play. We opened the traveler and we had a cold bottom. Watching from the dummy I'd been suffering, because I knew that he was misplaying the hand. The anger bubbled over. "I've never seen anyone mangle a hand that badly." I still remember my exact words.

Anyone who knows me today would be shocked if he heard me utter those words. Father Panek nipped the problem in the bud. After that session he gave me a pretty stern lecture about how to behave at the bridge table. He explained that I had embarrassed him, hurt his feelings, and thrown him off his game with that "mangling" speech. He made me understand that one must control his emotions at the table, and never say a harsh word to partner.

It may sound like an obvious and rudimentary lesson, but I cannot stress its importance. I do not wish to insult the reader, but I believe that very few people who are reading these words are able to behave at the table. We all have emotions, and they can be tough to control. If you promise yourself right now to try to change, you'll put your bridge career on the express train to success. Your partners will appreciate you and will consequently play better. When they can play without fear of criticism or retribution, they'll give you their A-game. You in turn will be in good spirits and give them your A-game. Furthermore, it makes for a friendlier and more enjoyable atmosphere for you and everyone else playing.

Choosing a Partner

Not everyone will be lucky enough to find a Father Panek. I was fortunate that he had the patience and tolerance to play with me, even though I was a novice. It was a tremendous learning experience to be playing with a better player. Furthermore, I was at an age where it was easy to absorb, and I didn't mind learning new conventions.

Nowadays, I'm reluctant to add lots of gadgets and science to the arsenal. I like to save my mind so that I can focus on the declarer play and defense. Picture a computer. There's only so much memory. If you load in one million bytes of bidding programs, there won't be any room for the program that plays the cards.

So if I had to look for a new partner today, I'd try to find someone with a similar mind set. "Don't load me up with conventions and science, pard — that's not me." Now some of you might prefer to have a full plate of conventions. No problem. But you've got to find a partner who thinks the same way; otherwise you'll feel held back.

My 10-year partnership with Marty Bergen ended primarily for that reason. He was a "mad-scientist" type, always wanting to amend the system notes. After every session we'd go over the boards and he'd want to change our methods. His suggestions always made sense, but I just simply didn't want to bog down my mind with constant changes and upgrades. Eventually our notes got to be so long and confusing that I couldn't take it anymore. Marty's dream partner would be someone like Eric Rodwell, who has the same penchant for unending science.

My present partner, David Berkowitz, is more on my wavelength. On the "convention/science scale" if "1" means you want to play only Stayman and Blackwood, and "10" means you want to play every artificial bid known to man, I'm probably a "4" and

David is a "5." Marty was a "9" or "10." There's no right way or wrong way, but you should try to choose a partner whose convention-scale rating is similar to yours.

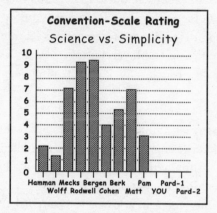

Add your rating and that of your two favorite partners.

First-time Partnerships vs. Longtime Partnerships

You'd expect that longtime partnerships have a big edge in any bridge tournament they enter. In general, that's true. There is one strange exception. It seems that the very first time two people play together, things often go better than expected. I attribute this to the fact that both players are on their very best behavior and try real hard. They want to make a good impression on the other player.

Also, nobody makes any "questionable bids or plays." For example, you're playing with Joe for the first time, and you hold:

♠ K x   ♡ K Q J 10 9 x   ◇ Q x x x   ♣ x

He deals and opens one spade and there is a two-club overcall on your right. You try two hearts and Joe gives you three diamonds.

LHO	Joe	RHO	You
—	1 ♠	2 ♣	2 ♡
pass	3 ◇	pass	?

Hmm. We have a pretty good hand here. Slam in diamonds or hearts is a real possibility opposite something like:

♠ A x x x x ♡ x ◇ A K x x ♣ A x x

Maybe we should cuebid four clubs. Maybe three hearts is forcing and will allow him to further describe his hand.

Forget those thoughts. We've never discussed this sort of auction with Joe. He might not think three hearts is forcing. Four clubs could lead to confusion. Why not just bid a simple four hearts and prevent a disaster? So you jump to four hearts, Joe passes with his ♠ A Q x x x ♡ x ◇ A J x x x ♣ Q x and you score up a game. You and Joe go on to have a nice, easy, pleasant session and score up 65%.

Now let's say that a person named Pamela, for instance, held that same ♠ K x ♡ K Q J 10 9 x ◇ Q x x x ♣ x.

She's playing with her partner of 16 years, Matthew. Matt opens one spade and Pamela bids two hearts after the two-club overcall. Matt bids three diamonds and it's up to Pamela. She remembers that she and Matt have discussed that if opener has bid a new suit at the three level after a two-over-one, he guarantees a rebid. So she bids three hearts (knowing that Matt will bid again) to leave room for slam exploration. Meanwhile, Matt remembers something else. He thinks back to the partnership rule that two-over-one is not game forcing, especially after an overcall. If responder rebids his suit (as in this case, two hearts and then three hearts), it is not forcing. So Matt passes and game is missed. It's not clear who was wrong — there seems to be two conflicting rules in the system notes. Pamela and Matthew have a little argument after this deal, and their session goes downhill from there. (This is a fictitious Pamela and Matthew, of course. The ones in this book would never spat at the table. They are too professional. Besides, they save all their arguments for their articles.)

Too Many Conventions?

Another advantage for new partnerships is that they don't play too many conventions. Say you're filling out a card with a new partner, and he asks, "Bergen Raises?" A good answer might be, "No thanks, there are too many variations and it involves too much discussion for now — let's just play natural limit raises." Down the road you agree to play conventions, but when they come up you'll often discover that you and partner are playing them differently!

So you understand now why Joe with his new partner will often do better than an experienced pair. Am I saying that a new partnership has an edge over an experienced one? No, of course not. I'm just trying to explain why first-time partners have such a high rate of success.

Conventionally Speaking

Speaking of conventions, what conventions should you play once you've decided to form a long-term partnership? There is no good answer to that one. If you want, you could read Amalya Kearse's classic reference book, "Bridge Conventions Complete," or more casually you could get a good overview by reading Marty Bergen's "Everyone's Guide to the New Convention Card" or the Granovetters' "Conventions at a Glance." (See also the Convention Check-List, page 138.) Of course, a lot will depend on you and your partner's aforementioned convention-scale rating. Don't start filling out a super-complex convention card if you are both 3's. Start your partnership out simply, even if you are 9's. Don't try to fill up your plate too fast — it's just not practical.

Most conventions have lots of ramifications, which take time to explore fully. If your new partnership agrees to play Bart, Lebensohl, Support Doubles, Good-Bad 2NT, and Roman Keycard Blackwood, you'll have tons of accidents. Conventions have many nuances. Agreeing to play "Keycard Blackwood" in itself is not enough. You must discuss if five clubs shows 0-3 or 1-4 keycards. How do you ask for kings? How do you ask for the trump queen? When is four notrump Keycard, as opposed to plain Blackwood or quantitative? What is the trump suit — is it the last bid suit or the first agreed suit? Is there always a trump suit? And so on. (See page 130.) A similar array of questions could be attached to almost any convention. "What do we do if they interfere over our convention?" "Is it on in competition?" "Is it on opposite a passed hand?" etc.

Partners That Kiss

Ever hear of the KISS system? It's an acronym I believe in. Keep It Simple, Stupid.

I know lots of people (and I'm afraid I'm one of them) who were so fascinated when they were learning bridge that they tried to write down and define every auction. I spent many hours in college defining bridge auctions instead of taking notes on the lecture.

Unfortunately, no matter how diligent and thorough you are, you simply can't define every auction. There are millions of them. Even if you could define every auction, how could you possibly remember your definitions? Therefore, I've resolved to go the simple route. I try not to designate meanings for too many auctions. Bridge players are not computers. It's best to Keep It Simple!

 Here-and-there methods

Auctions always come up where your partner might say, "Hey, I know a gimmick for this. We can play that a jump in their suit to the four level asks for . . ." Just forget it. Don't add "Here-and-there" methods. I call a "Here-and-there" method one that was invented just to handle a specific situation that occurred at the table. You put it in your system, and then it doesn't come up for five years. By then, nobody remembers it anymore. Don't add methods unless they are for handling useful, recurring hand-types.

A Final Kiss from a Reformed Scientist

In all of my partnerships I like to develop a nice, natural, uncomplicated system. Sure, I might add a few gadgets, but the framework is always mundane: five-card majors, weak two-bids, negative doubles, natural bidding! I've had my flings with Multi, Transfer Preempts, Relays, etc. Once I even tried to learn a Strong-pass system, where an "opening" pass showed 16 or more points. Talk about artificiality! The memory strain just ain't worth it.

Besides, I think it's best for the game of bridge to use natural bidding. If the game is ever to attract large masses or become a spectator sport, we've got to make it understandable. Joe Citizen is not going to follow what's going on if every bid is alertable. I take pride in the fact that David and I play a basically natural system. Yes, we play Precision, which uses an artificial one-club opening, but almost all of our follow-ups are natural. When we are on VuGraph or have kibitzers, everyone can follow what's going on.

If you're a 19-year old physics major at M.I.T. with a photo-graphic memory, and you have a similar partner, then by all means fill out the most complicated system card that you dare to. If you're anyone else, do yourself a favor and stick to the basics: KISS.

Chapter 11: Work and Learn

A good partnership takes work. Sorry, but there's no way around it, and no substitute for it. With any serious partner there are three chores that I consider a must:

(1) Maintain partnership bidding/system notes.

(2) Practice bidding hands before important events.

(3) Go over the boards at the end of the day.

David and I take our partnership very seriously. A substantial part of our income is derived from playing professionally on teams at the nationals. We get paid good money, and we feel an obligation to be prepared. Aside from the above three work requirements, we do everything else we can to give the team sponsor our best effort. We get to sleep on time the night before an important match (no partying or late nights out drinking), and we don't eat big meals before playing. Between sessions we go to our hotel room and relax. No strenuous bridge talk, and no boisterous dinner with cocktails. This is not necessarily a requirement for a partnership, but it's nice to know that David and I feel the same way about this subject.

The next three sections cover the above-mentioned "chores."

(1) Partnership Bidding/System Notes

The computer age has been a boon in this area. Years ago it was rare to find partnerships with a full set of notes. It was a pain to have various sheets of paper (tattered and frayed) with changes and cross-outs. In the late 1970's I formed a successful partnership with Ron Gerard. He was a lawyer, and he'd always write up detailed system notes on those long yellow sheets of legal paper. He'd mail them to me at college, and I'd study them more than my textbooks. I ended up with stacks of these yellow pages, and after a while it became unwieldy — there was no good way to organize them.

Nowadays you just need a word-processing program (a little bit of page-layout knowledge is nice) and you're in business. Current statistics show that 50% of ACBL members own computers, so there's a good chance that you or your partner have access.

You first must decide how much information should go in the notes. Should you just keep a list of difficult-to-remember things? Should you list what every single bid means, even a one-heart opening bid? Where do you draw the line?

I've tried many different schemes, so I'll pass on to you what I think is the best route. I like to write down almost everything.

Your first page should be a table of contents, perhaps as follows:

 Beware of system updates

Pamela: We spent our first year working on 13 pages of system notes and vowed never to make a change.

Matthew: One day I added a few wrinkles. . . .

Pamela: After our 40% game, we incorporated a new policy: one update permitted every leap year.

System Notes
Table of Contents

The letters "a-r" are, of course, the page numbers. If you're Meckstroth and Rodwell, they might run into the 800's. David and I don't even make it out of the double-digit area. Most top partnerships (the best 10 pairs in the country) have anywhere from 50 to 200 pages of such notes. I'd estimate that 20 to 30 pages are more than sufficient for most partnerships.

Let's take a quick look at what might be listed within these pages.

In the Opening-Bids section the only things of consequence might be bids starting with three notrump and higher. Everything else is probably easy to remember.

For One-of-a-minor Openings and Responses, I'd write a brief line or two about the requirements for one club vs. one diamond, and I'd also briefly list all the responses (Walsh style or up-the-line; what the ranges are for 1NT, 2NT, and 3NT responses; what are jump-shifts? what is three-of-a-major? etc.). From there, I'd talk about any further agreements, such as what opener's bids mean after 1◊-2♣. (See page 32.)

Things such as new-minor forcing, negative doubles, bids-in-competition, I would list on "Page g" in the Table of Contents. And there's no reason to repeat agreements for the one-of-a-minor section in the one-of-a-major section.

In the Opening Notrump section, I would list the range (not that you're likely to forget), and all of the first-round responses, even Stayman. Then I'd go into more detail about Stayman follow-ups, transfer follow-ups, etc. You'd also discuss two-notrump (and if natural, three-notrump) openings in this space. This could be a very long section for serious partnerships. The section Over Interference is also very important. Don't forget to put in all agreements if one notrump is doubled.

In Other Openings, you'd write all your agreements over the various opening bids (such as unusual two-bids and higher openings), somewhat mirroring the information you'd put on your convention card. In fact, you've probably noticed that all my headings approximate the order of the convention card.

The Opponents Open One of a Suit section takes up plenty of room in my notes. There are all sorts of partnership agreements that develop, for example:

1) Our direct cuebids (Michaels) and unusual notrump and follow-ups.

2) Our one-notrump overcall and follow-ups.
   • What to do if we're doubled.

3) Our takeout doubles.
   • What are cuebids by responder to the double?
   • How high are we forced?
   • Equal-level conversion principles.
   • Responsive doubles.
   • Methods after they redouble.
   • Strengths involved for doubling and raising.
   • What it means to double and convert a jump to notrump.
   • And more. . . .

4) Balancing one-notrump strengths (after various openings) and follow-ups.

5) Our overcalls.
   • Are new suits forcing?
   • What are jump responses and raises?
   • When can we make a forcing pass, if ever? (See page 58.)
   • What is a jump-cue response?
   • How do we follow-up when advancer cuebids in response to the overcall?
   • What are jump overcalls in the balancing seat, especially two notrump.
   • And more. . . . .

6) Agreements after they've opened and raised.
   • What is two notrump?
   • How light can we double?
   • And more. . . .

My notes with David on this section are six full pages. These are the kinds of agreements that new partnerships don't have, but experienced ones must have.

> **Note:** Are you wondering why my notes have all this "junk"? After all, I said that I like to Keep It Simple. Simple and "thorough" are two different things. Our notes are not filled with complicated artificial gadgets. Instead, they are filled with partnership agreements about commonly occurring events. The longer you play with a partner, the more such "events" you can discuss. Items in the #1-6 list on the last page aren't complex, but they all involve auctions that come up in the day-to-day battles, and I like to know that my partner and I will be on the same wavelength. Definitions involving these routine situations take up most of the pages.

As you continue to fill in your notes you'll notice some areas of duplication, especially in the Slam Conventions section. For example, splinter bids could go in the slam section as well as under one-of-a-major. Here are some of the subtitles you might want in the slam section: Roman Keycard Blackwood (with a subheading for Trump-Queen asks and Exclusion Blackwood); Grand Slam Force; 5NT Pick-a-Slam; DoPi; Jumps to the 5-level; Cuebidding; Asking Bids; 4NT Quantitative.

Carding is probably the most overlooked and under-emphasized area of partnership. It reminds me of golfers that spend 95% of their time practicing drivers and long-iron shots on the range, but never work on their putting or chipping. Defensive carding will come into play on about half the deals you play. Any good partnership should spend time discussing as many aspects as possible. Here are the major areas, with some of my suggestions and ideas:

A) General Philosophy

You must decide if in general you are giving attitude or count (I prefer attitude). Also, the overall general concept should be to show where your values are. I stress this, because I've often heard defenders say, "I shifted to a diamond because you asked me for one." This is not the right outlook. Instead, the signal should be "showing diamond values." Then it is up to the person receiving the signal to decide whether to shift to diamonds. For example:

```
South dealer      North
N-S vul           ♠ 10 x x
                  ♡ Q x
                  ◇ A Q x
                  ♣ A K Q x x
West                              East
♠ x x                            ♠ J x
♡ A K J x                        ♡ 8 7 5 4 2
◇ 10 x x x                       ◇ K J x
♣ J x x                          ♣ x x x
                  South
                  ♠ A K Q 9 x x
                  ♡ x x
                  ◇ x x x
                  ♣ x x
```

After opening two spades at matchpoints, South becomes declarer in four spades and West leads a high heart. East signals with the deuce — he can stand a diamond switch. West duly switches to a diamond and South takes 12 tricks. "You asked me for a switch," screams West. No, East was simply showing that he could stand a diamond switch. Armed with that knowledge, West should still try to cash his other heart. He can see that a diamond switch could easily result in 12 tricks.

So in a good partnership, signals should be used to show your hand, not for masterminding (or dictating) the defense.

B) Opening Leads

This is covered by filling out the convention card, but notable areas are what to lead against notrump from big holdings such as A-K-J-10-x. Some people play that the ace asks for one signal, and the king for a different one.

C) Trick One

Signaling at trick one is a topic that longtime partnerships are still working on. Entire books (like the Granovetters' A Switch in Time) have been written about this complex topic.

D) Signals and Leads During the Hand

This is also covered on the convention card, but special partnership tendencies and agreements develop throughout the years. For example, would you shift to a high, low, or medium club from 8-7-4-2 if leading through declarer at notrump? The answer could be that it depends on the rest of the deal. Another example: Some people play that against notrump the lead of the 10 promises a higher honor. Some play this after trick one as well.

E) Other Methods

These include Smith Echo, odd-even, and suit-preference. There are tons of concepts to discuss, and this is an area where the truly great partnerships have a big advantage. Almost every little card on defense means something. There are constant inferences to be drawn because your expert partner has followed with the 2-5-7 in that order as opposed to the 2-7-5.

I've had many discussions with my partner (usually after letting three notrump make) that sound something like this:

Larry: "I wasn't sure if this was a Smith-Echo situation."

Partner: "Yeah, me too. Since dummy seemed to have spades stopped, I didn't think you could show spades."

Larry: "I agree. Also, I thought you might need count, since it wasn't clear if declarer could get back to dummy."

Partner: "Well, it looked like he had a spade entry, but only if he had a spade left in hand. So I guess we should assume in these situations that if a high card is in dummy, it is indeed an entry and, therefore, we should give count in the side suit."

Larry: "OK. And remember that with 9-8-3-2 we give count with the 8. The 3 followed by the 2 would show the doubleton. Always the second highest from four."

Of course, these conversations take place long after the session has ended.

(2) Practice Bidding Hands Before Important Events

This is another area where the computer has become a big help. Random-deal generators are commonplace in the market, and most top partnerships own one. Before important events I think it's a good idea to practice.

One way to practice is to play. I find this less effective than computer-generated bidding hands. True, most people find it more enjoyable to play bridge than to sit there bidding hands, but it just doesn't get the job done as well. In a typical tournament you play 52 to 56 deals a day, and your side doesn't even have bidding decisions on about one third of those deals. By bidding off practice sheets we can do 50 deals in a few hours. Not only that, we can learn a lot by "talking" during our practice bidding. "I'm bidding three hearts, but I'm curious about what you think it would have meant if I had jumped to four hearts. Is three hearts forcing? etc."

We sometimes deal out random hands, but at other times we set up the deals so that we can practice a certain area of bidding.

Perhaps we've made a recent change to our responses to one notrump, so we'll deal out 100 notrump openers and bid those hands.

We're also able to practice our competitive bidding. No, we don't get two other players, so you might wonder how we do it! Simple. We tell the computer to print out, say, 25 deals where the East-West hands have an eight-card (or longer) heart fit. My partner and I then take the North-South hands, and we "give ourselves" heart interference. For example, I pick up the first North hand and open one club. "It goes two hearts on your right," I tell David. Then we continue bidding. On the next deal I might tell him, "They overcall one heart, and then jump-raise to three hearts." We continue through all 25 hands, and whoever feels like it makes up the opponents' actions. Sometimes we pretend they opened two hearts or three hearts. This is quite an effective method for practicing competitive bidding, and you'll probably discover some better refinements as you go along.

The only drawback to practice bidding rather than actual playing is that we don't get to work on our defense and signaling. (Declarer play is practiced by reading books — you don't need a partner to practice this aspect!) What we sometimes do is look at old printouts of hand records and discuss how we would signal and defend. We also read lots of books and magazine articles, always keeping an eye open for a defensive situation that we should discuss.

> **Editors' Note:** Beware of practicing with hands from magazine bidding challenges, unless they come from a real tournament. Usually you'll find too many trick hands, where the best bidding still leads to the wrong contract. These challenges may be fun for casual bidding over lunch, but they will depress you when, for example, you can't stay out of a hopeless three notrump with 26 points between the two hands.

(3) Go Over the Boards at the End of the Day

This might not mean what you think it does. The typical post-mortem session involves a bunch of people sitting around laughing and partying. "What'd you do on Board 7?" "You wouldn't believe what this guy did against us!" I'm not talking about a social hour. Sure, it's fun to sit around after the session and tell stories, but there's another kind of fun as well: the fun of improving.

What I mean by going over the boards is that just you and your partner sit in a quiet, studious atmosphere. It should be a private, almost intimate thing. You don't want other people around. You start with board one and your attitude should be: "Did anything happen in the bidding or play that I wanted to discuss with partner?" Whether you got a top or a bottom, you might want to ask about a certain bid or play, or even a hypothetical bid or play. "What would it have meant if . . ." "I wanted to signal you for a club shift, but I was afraid I'd be giving count. . . ." "Did we change the meaning of jumps to the four level on this auction?" "How could I have told you to cash out?"

This exchange of ideas must be done maturely. It's a sensitive area, and you've got to set your ego aside. Try to adopt an attitude of "What could I have done better to help my partner?" Don't try to explain to your partner what he should have done. Ask not what your partner should do for you, but what you could do for your partner.

Chapter 12: Troubleshooting

Let's take a look at four important trouble areas in building a partnership: Keeping Your Mouth Shut During the Session, Zig-zagging, Misunderstandings, and Bidding Rules.

Keep Your Mouth Shut During the Session

Hamman and Wolff are the absolute best. I've never seen them say a word during a session of bridge. Even after the world's worst bidding misunderstanding they both have totally unruffled looks; not a word is exchanged. You don't know which one of them made the mistake, and they don't seem to care. It's on to the next board.

It's very difficult to do what they do. Everyone's natural impulse is to say, "Sorry, I thought that four notrump was Blackwood," or "I would have passed, but I thought it was forcing."

It does absolutely no good to make such statements. Even if your intentions and tone of voice are good, you should keep quiet instead. When you say, "I thought four notrump was Blackwood," your partner will hear, "You dimwit, didn't you know that four notrump is Blackwood on this auction?" When you say, "I thought is was forcing," she'll hear, "You didn't know our system."

You just can't win. Many, many times I've seen players of all levels initiate a postmortem only to have it cause partnership disharmony. Think back to all of your uncomfortable moments at the table with partner — don't they all stem from postmortems? Because the atmosphere is so intense (especially after a bad result), even the nicest and most innocent comments often lead to argument and dissension.

Furthermore, it usually pumps up the opponents when you and your partner discuss your bad results. Especially in a long team match, I know that I get an extra boost when my opponents are having trouble. When I get a good result against Hamman-Wolff and they just shrug it off and go on to the next deal, I don't feel any momentum. However, when Frick and Frack are going at each other, stewing in the unpleasantness of their minus 800, I feel an extra burst of energy kick in, and I'm ready to slaughter them on the next board as well. It's just the natural competitive nature of a bridge player. So don't give your opponents that same satisfaction!

Listen here, pard; take a lesson from the world's best pairs, and keep your mouth shut.

Zigzagging

Our teammates once landed in a 3-3 fit, because they were on the wrong wavelength. Mike held:

♠ A x ♡ K Q x ◊ A 9 8 x ♣ K x x x

and with both vulnerable at imps he heard one diamond on his right. He overcalled one notrump. His partner, Paul, bid two diamonds, a transfer to hearts. Mike bid two hearts and Paul jumped to three notrump. Naturally, Mike converted this to four hearts, and this caused Paul some consternation. After long thought Paul passed, and tabled:

♠ K Q x x ♡ J x x ◊ 10 x ♣ A x x x

The 3-3 fit didn't fare too well, down two, cold for three notrump. What happened?

The pair had recently decided to play two-way Stayman after one-notrump overcalls. Paul had remembered, but Mike hadn't. Paul thought of going back to four notrump, but hoped instead that Mike somehow had a five-card heart suit.

Our team lost 12 imps on the board, but since we went on to win the match, we were all able to laugh about the 3-3 fit. Paul reminded Mike that they had recently agreed to change to forcing Stayman (only after one-notrump overcalls). Mike said that he thinks it's a silly method — that's why he had trouble remembering.

Anyway, several months later, Paul held:

♠ K Q x ♡ Q x x x ◇ A x ♣ K Q x x

and heard one-club on his right. He overcalled one notrump and Mike bid two diamonds. Already Paul was worried. Had Mike remembered correctly this time? Paul responded two hearts to Stayman and Mike jumped to three notrump — same situation as last time but different seats. A wave of doubt flashed through Paul's head. Didn't Mike say he hates two-way Stayman? Paul decided that Mike was transferring to hearts, so Paul bid four hearts. This time it was Mike who looked perplexed, but eventually he passed. The 4-2 fit did not succeed.

This brings to mind a famous saying. "Fool me once, shame on you. Fool me twice, shame on me." Any partnership is going to have misunderstandings. There's no way to avoid them. The key is to avoid a repeat of a mix-up. I told Mike and Paul, "I forgive you for the first one, but for God's sake, get it straightened out so that you are on the same page next time."

Don't zigzag. If you are on a different wavelength from your partner, that's OK. But after the session get it ironed out. Agree to do it one way or the other. Play two-way Stayman (Paul's way) or Jacoby transfers (Mike's way). You've got to get on the same page.

Misunderstandings

You're sailing along having a good session and all of a sudden a misunderstanding occurs. The opponents overcall hearts in front of you, and raise them on your left. In a competitive auction, your partner bids three hearts, which you think shows a stopper. You try three notrump and everyone passes. Let's review:

LHO	Partner	RHO	You
—	1 ♢	1 ♡	2 ♣
2 ♡	3 ♡	pass	3 NT
(all pass)			

A heart is led. You have Q-x of hearts and dummy has two small. First of all, when dummy hits, you must speak no evil and see no evil. Act as calm as can be. If you start yelling or complaining or looking disgusted, the opponents will run the suit in no time. As it turns out, RHO has A-K-9-x-x of hearts and lefty has led a low heart from J-10-x-x. Third hand decides that you have ♡Q-10-x, so he wins the heart lead and then underleads, hoping you'll stick in the 10. Instead your queen wins and you make your contract.

Lesson 1: Don't ever show emotion when the dummy hits. Always act confident.

Now, let's assume you have the same hand and the same auction. You still smile when the dummy hits, but the opponents are not confused — they quickly run five heart tricks for down one and you get a bottom. Should you say anything nasty to your partner? Should you rant and rave? Should you try to clear up the misunderstanding? The answers are: No, No, and Later.

Lesson 2: Do not discuss bridge during the session.

Why wait until later? Maybe you need to clear this up in case it comes up again in the same session. Forget it. It's extremely unlikely to come up again in that session or that day or that week or month. It's much more likely that your discussion will upset the spirit of the partnership.

Usually after a bad result from a misunderstanding both players are fuming inside. They each think their interpretation is correct. In the example above, dummy is sure his three-heart bid asked for a stopper, and you're sure that it showed one. In the heat of battle, neither you nor your partner will want to admit that he is wrong.

The end of the day is the time to clear these things up. If you simply must, you can ask some experts their opinion, and then form your partnership agreement accordingly. I don't recommend this tactic. No one likes to hear, "I asked Paul Soloway, and he says that my interpretation was correct, and yours was wrong!" Try to logically work out an agreement with your partner, add it to your notes (if you have them) and go on from there.

What if something comes up during the session and you're afraid that you'll forget to bring it up later? Just make a note on your scorecard. After a typical session I usually have three or four little notes jotted down. Either I write down the board numbers, or something like "1C-1H-1S-4D—double for diamonds."* It doesn't have to be a misunderstanding that causes you to make notes. If you're like me, lots of "what if's" will pop into your head during an auction. No problem occurs on the actual deal, but you'd like to ask your partner what such-and-such would have meant.

I repeat. Do not resolve it at the table or during the session. Talk to your partner about anything other than bridge. Talk about romance, sports, sex, or politics (well, maybe not politics). You'll have a much better time and you'll keep the partnership in the proper spirit.

Bidding Rules

So you've agreed on your basic conventions. You have your card filled out, and you know that you play 2/1 game force, two-way Stayman, five-card majors with limit raises, negative doubles

---

*We play that the double of a splinter requests the lead of the highest ranking unbid suit. In this case, all the suits were bid, so I jotted down a note to confirm with my partner that this double is for diamonds.

through three spades, DONT over their notrump, Roman Keycard Blackwood (0-3, 1-4 — you did discuss that, right?), and fourth-best leads. Maybe a few other gadgets like new-minor forcing, weak jumps in competition, etc.

A year or two goes by and you want to put in some fancier stuff. You decide to add some bids that ask for shortness. One of you has heard of "Mathe asking bids." They occur after 1M-3M, a limit raise, or after any substitute for a limit raise, such as 1♠-3◇ showing a limit raise. The next step asks for shortness.

So with ♠ x x x ♡ A K x x x x ◇ A ♣ K Q x, you open one heart and partner limit raises to three hearts. You ask with three spades and partner shows spade shortness. This delights you no end, and you Blackwood to slam and find ♠ x ♡ Q J x x ◇ K x x x ♣ A x x x.

All well and good, but how did your partner show the spade shortness? You asked with three spades, and if he had no shortness he would have signed-off in four hearts. To show shortness in clubs, diamonds, or spades he had three bids available: three notrump, four clubs, and four diamonds. When you agreed to play Mathe asking bids, did you remember to discuss how you would actually show the shortness? This is an inherent flaw with adding conventions (see page 107, "Agreements You Won't Find on the Convention Card"). Unless you discuss them thoroughly, there is room for misunderstanding.

So what should it be? Clearly four hearts should show no shortness. Should three notrump (first available step) show short-ness in the lowest suit, clubs? And then the next step, four clubs shows shortness in diamonds, and then four diamonds is shortness in the highest suit, spades? Or you could play that four clubs and four diamonds show natural shortness in that suit, and three notrump is used as a "replacement" to show short spades. I say "replace-ment" because you don't want to bid four spades (getting past four hearts) to show spade shortness. So which will it be, "Up-the-line" or "Natural with replacement?"

Pick one. There are theoretical implications as to which is better, but that's beyond the scope of this discussion.

A few months go by, and you decide to add a wrinkle to your weak two-bids. You play that after partner opens a weak two, three clubs asks for shortness (a somewhat popular method). Remember, you must also decide how to answer the ask! Say it goes 2♡-3♣. Clearly, three hearts should say "no shortness." What about three diamonds, three spades, and three notrump. Is it "Up-the line" or "Natural with replacement?" If it's "Up-the line," three diamonds is club shortness (cheapest suit), three spades is diamond short-ness, and three notrump is spade shortness. If "Natural with re-placement," three diamonds and three spades show natural short-ness in that suit, and three notrump is replacement to show club shortness.

Again, there are theoretical reasons to play it one way or the other. But there is a huge reason to decide how you should play it. You should play it the same way as you chose to use over Mathe asking bids. Don't play it one way over Mathe, and the other over weak twos, because you think there is a good reason. It's too much memory strain.

Let me elaborate a bit on this important point. Even if you don't care about the conventions I'm using for my examples, the overrid-ing principle will be of relevance.

There are a few things (very few) that I think are worthy of exceptions. Here's one example. You and your regular partner have agreements on what you should do when the opponents jump overcall with an unusual two notrump. Most people play some variation of what is called "Unusual over Unusual." You open one heart and LHO bids two notrump for the minors. Now, three spades is natural and nonforcing, and three hearts is a heart raise, but with a minimum. "Cuebids" of three clubs and three diamonds are used to show the forcing spade hand, and a good raise of hearts. As to which one is which, that's up to you. Some people play "Low-to

Low/High to High" (3♣ = hearts, 3◊ = spades) while others play that the first step always shows the "other" suit (after a 1♡ opening, 3♣ = spades, 3◊ = hearts).

Again, without going into the science, there are theoretical reasons why you should play it one way as opposed to the other. The best way is to use the first step to show the forcing hand in the "other" suit, and the second step to show a good raise. So let's assume you have that agreement. You open one spade and they bid two notrump for the minors. Now, three clubs shows a forcing heart hand (first step for "other" suit), and three diamonds shows a good (limit) raise in spades.

So what has this got to do with exceptions? Say you open one diamond and LHO bids two notrump to show the two lowest unbid suits (clubs and hearts). Using our partnership rules, a bid of three clubs (step one) would show a forcing hand in spades (the "other" suit). A bid of three hearts (step 2) would show a good (limit) raise in diamonds. But that doesn't make sense. Our three-heart bid (limit raise) has taken us past three diamonds. It doesn't seem right to have a limit raise take us past our "limit." For that reason, my partner and I invert our normal meanings when it goes 1◊-2NT. We hate to have exceptions, but this is one we're willing to make.

It's one of the rare exceptions. We used to have lots of other such exceptions and "flip-flops." We used to invert meanings on lots of auctions. We'd use an artificial response in notrump to show a certain feature so that they couldn't double for the lead. We'd invert our responses to Blackwood on certain auctions in order to stay below five of the trump suit. But eventually we gave it all up.

Meckstroth and Rodwell, often considered the world's best pair, play the world's most complex bidding system. They can do it. They've played together for 20 years in thousands of events. They play together for a living, study their notes constantly, and have great memories. (Even so, they have their share of mix-ups.) Rodwell is very scientific, and a great bidding theoretician. He wants all of their partnership agreements to be thought out to perfection. Even if it causes a memory problem, he wants to be playing methods that are theoretically best.

Therefore, you'll find lots of "exceptions" in their system notes. For example, in many auctions, they play step bids, the lowest bid corresponding to clubs and so forth. But sometimes they change the order if the logic of the auction dictates. I hate exceptions. To me they're confusing. I'd rather stick to a general rule for all auctions and sacrifice a slight bit of accuracy in exchange for not having any misunderstandings. I'm a simple soul, and I'd rather stick to "up-the-line" artificial bidding: step one for clubs, step two for diamonds, etc., even if it isn't theoretically perfect.

If you and your partner are real scientists with great memories, by all means load yourself up with rules and exceptions to the rules. But for 99% of you out there, I'd say, "Forget the exceptions." David and I have had plenty of success with our modest set of rules. Every now and then we have a theoretical inadequacy in our auctions, but we don't mind paying the price. We hardly ever have misunderstandings, and it's only one time in 100 that the deficiency hurts us anyway. We don't have to study pages and pages of exceptions, and we will live longer and more prosperous lives.

Cherish Your Partner

I can't say it enough, so I'll say it again. You've got to keep your partner happy, especially during the session. Whatever it takes, remember to keep a smile on your face and a pleasant attitude. Do not accuse, yell at, frown at, complain to, criticize, castigate, disparage, abuse, ridicule, sneer at, or mock your partner. Try to be comforting, supportive, compassionate, encouraging, reassuring, sympathetic, and understanding.

This might sound simple, but it's not. It's so easy to get hot under the collar, especially when things go wrong. You're dying for a spade switch and you've obviously signaled for one. The caddie, the kibitzer, and Stevie Wonder would know to shift to a spade, but that imbecile called partner shifts to a heart — minus 790. You're ready to slam your fist through the table (or partner's face) or burst a blood vessel. It's not easy to maintain your composure.

But this is the time that you must step up to the plate and show your stuff. Keep a calm face, don't say a word. Partner might apologize (that's permitted), or he might wonder what was wrong with your signal! He might think it's your fault. But he too should keep a calm demeanor. Maybe you can apologize, even though you "know" it's not your fault. After the session you can figure out what went wrong, preferably in private. Don't argue with your partner in front of other people.

And, especially, don't talk negatively about your partner behind his back. Again, this is easier said than done. You've had a 57% game, but you just know that it would have been 60% if partner had made that six-spade contract. A friend asks you how you did. Your answer should be "We had a good game," or "decent, could have been better." Not, "Would have had 60% if that dope hadn't gone down in a cold slam." Even if you do survive this hurdle, don't give the six-spade hand as a play problem to your friends.

Note: Concerning teammates, the words "behind their back" are key. Don't malign them. Just like you should be a good partner, you should be a good teammate. Hardly any of us are. How often we have heard: "Would have won with any other pair on the planet at the other table, but not those two morons," or "Every time our opponents bid and made a game we lost 10 imps." Anyway, you know what I'm talking about.

My final advice is this: Be a good teammate and a good partner — the one you'll be helping the most is yourself!

Part III. Partnership Check-Lists

Chapter 13: Agreements You Won't Find on the Convention Card

— 70 Items to Discuss With Your Partner —

Everyone fills out the convention card, but do you and partner discuss your conventions thoroughly? Here are some of the most common agreements (sometimes referred to as "treatments") that almost every long-standing partnership has discussed. A couple of these have actually been added to the new ACBL convention card.

You should discuss all of these points with your partner and agree how you will play them. The ideas here are the most popular methods; when we (Pamela and Matthew) disagree with the popular method, we present our preference. You can choose to play these bids any way you like; the most important thing is to be sure both players agree.

One-Notrump Auctions

1. After Stayman is doubled, how do you proceed?

West	North	East	South
1 NT	pass	2 ♣	double
?			

Redouble by either player is a strong desire to play in two clubs redoubled.

Pass by opener is simply waiting to hear from partner, who may redouble to play or make a nonforcing bid at the two level or natural force at the three level. Three clubs is Stayman (again).

The bids of 2◊, 2♡, or 2♠ by opener are the same as if there were no double.

Note: You may wish to play, as we do, that with weak clubs opener will pass even though he holds a four-card major. This allows responder to declare in the 4-4 fit with a club tenace, such as ♣K-x opposite opener's ♣x-x-x. Responder bids 2♡ or 2♠ now with a four-card major, forcing one round.

2. If you play "nonforcing Stayman" (i.e., responder's rebid at the two level is not forcing), decide how you play the rebid of 2♡ or 2♠, weak or invitational.

West	North	East	South
1 NT	pass	2 ♣	pass
2 ◊	pass	2 ♡	

Most play this as very weak, asking opener to choose a major. We prefer the rebid of 2♡ or 2♠ as mildly invitational.

Transfers:
3. When a transfer is doubled, acceptance by opener shows three-card support, and a redouble by either partner shows a strong desire to play it right there.

West	North	East	South
1 NT	pass	2 ◊	double
?			

2 ♡ = heart support
redouble = let's play in 2◊ redoubled

4. The transfer to 2♡ and rebid of 2♠ is often used conventionally.

West	North	East	South
1 NT	pass	2 ◇	pass
2 ♡	pass	2 ♠	

What does this mean to you? You decide.

5. Transfer at the two level followed by 4NT is quantitative. Texas followed by 4NT is Keycard Blackwood. Texas followed by a new suit is Exclusion Keycard Blackwood (a void in the suit bid).

West	North	East	South
1 NT	pass	2 ♡	pass
2 ♠	pass	4 NT = invites slam	

West	North	East	South
1 NT	pass	4 ♡	pass
4 ♠	pass	?	

4 NT = Keycard Blackwood, spades are trumps

5 ♣ = Keycard Blackwood, don't count the ♣A

5 ◇ = Keycard Blackwood, don't count the ◇A

5 ♡ = Keycard Blackwood, don't count the ♡A

6. Do you play Texas after interference? Most play that Texas is ON after second seat doubles or overcalls through 3♣.

West	North	East	South
1 NT	3 ♣	4 ◇ = transfer to hearts	

West	North	East	South
1 NT	3 ◇	4 ◇ = Stayman	

7. After interference, there are a number of problems to solve:

West	North	East	South
1 NT	2 ♠	double	

The majority of partnerships still use penalty doubles, though the negative-double crowd is gaining fast. We use penalty at the two level, negative at the three level.

West	North	East	South
1 NT	pass	pass	2 ♠
double			

Most play this as penalty and if West passes, East's double is also penalty.

Lebensohl:

8. This is the popular method after an overcall. The bid of 2NT transfers to clubs to get out somewhere or show a good hand with a stopper in their suit. The direct cuebid or 3NT denies a stopper. This treatment is known as "Slow shows, direct denies:"

West	North	East	South
1 NT	2 ♠	2 NT	pass
3 ♣	pass	?	

3♠ = Stayman showing a spade stopper
3NT = A raise to game showing a spade stopper

West	North	East	South
1 NT	2 ♠	?	

3♠ = Stayman denying a spade stopper
3NT = a raise to game denying a spade stopper

We prefer to play transfers at the three level after they overcall, with a simple cuebid for Stayman. This method does not show or deny stoppers, but has the advantage of making the 1NT opener the declarer when responder has a long suit. Here is the structure:

West	North	East	South
1 NT	2 ♠	?	

2 NT = natural
3 ♣ = transfer to diamonds
3 ◇ = transfer to hearts
3 ♡ = transfer to clubs
3 ♠ = Stayman

West	North	East	South
1 NT	2 ♡	?	

2 ♠ = natural
2 NT = natural
3 ♣ = transfer to diamonds
3 ◇ = transfer to spades
3 ♡ = Stayman
3 ♠ = transfer to clubs

9. When 1NT is doubled:

West	North	East	South
1 NT	double	?	

Whatever that double means, the popular method is "System On." Ignore the double and continue, with the additional call of redouble as a strong balanced hand. This system also applies after a 2♣ overcall, using a double for Stayman.

10. Against weak notrumps, play that the double of Stayman shows a strong hand — nothing to do with clubs. This is because weak notrumpers like to respond 2♣ with weak hands to try to avoid a penalty double by fourth seat.

West	North	East	South
1 NT*	pass	2 ♣	double = good hand

*weak, 12-14 (or 10-12)

2NT Opening or 2NT rebid after 2♣

11. Stayman followed by the other major is a slam try in opener's major.

West	North	East	South
2 NT	pass	3 ♣	pass
3 ♠	pass	4 ♡ = slam try in spades	

12. The popular method to show a one-suit slam try in a major is to transfer at the three level and raise to four, while the direct transfer at the four level is weak. This method is definitely inferior to the reverse idea: The direct Texas transfer is the slam try.

West	North	East	South
2 NT	pass	3 ◊	pass
3 ♡	pass	4 ♡	

West	North	East	South
2 NT	pass	4 ◊	

The first auction is usually played as a slam try, while the second is a shutout bid in hearts. The theoretically superior method is the reverse, because by transferring at the three level with a medium hand, you allow opener to express slam interest. Nevertheless, you should choose the method that you will remember.

3NT Openings

13. The opening bid of 3NT is usually played as Gambling, a solid minor and little outside. Responder's 4♣ tells partner to pass or correct to diamonds; responder's 4◇ asks for a singleton.

West	North	East	South
3 NT	pass	4 ◇	pass
?			

4NT = no singleton
5m = natural, singleton in the other minor

We play the opening 3NT also shows an outside honor. Almost everyone plays it this way in third or fourth seat.

Major-Suit Openings

14. Do you play two-over-one forcing to game? If not (we don't), review the ways responder can make a nonforcing rebid.

West	North	East	South
1 ♠	pass	2 ♣	pass
2 ◇	pass	?	

We play 2♠ and 3♣ are the only nonforcing bids. You and your partner should review this and decide which rebids are nonforcing.

15. What does opener's jump mean after a two-over-one?

West	North	East	South
1 ♠	pass	2 ♣	pass
3 ♡ = ?			

The popular method is to play the jump as a splinter in support of clubs. We like the old-fashioned, natural meaning: a strong 5-5.

16. Do you play "fast arrival" or "slow arrival"? For example:

West	North	East	South
1 ♠	pass	2 ♡	pass
4 ♡ = ?			

If you play this jump as a weak hand, you play the more fashionable "fast arrival." We prefer that a jump in trumps shows mild slam interest with strong trumps. We play "slow arrival."

Just like a jump to four of a minor by West would show a slam try with a singleton, the jump to game in hearts shows a slam try without a singleton. The reason for "slow arrival" is that when East holds a good hand with a bad heart suit, he won't initiate a slam try over a raise to 3♡. He needs to hear about the strong trumps.

These principles apply only when the raise to the three level is forcing. Another instance occurs when West rebids 2♠ and East raises to 4♠. If 3♠ is forcing, the jump to 4♠ shows something like:
♠ A K x x ♡ A Q 10 x x ◇ x x ♣ x x.

 #1 on the top-10 chart of disaster-prone sequences

West	North	East	South
1 ♡	pass	4 NT	

Do you play Keycard Blackwood? Is 4NT Keycard for hearts? Or is it plain Blackwood? If you can raise hearts first and then Blackwood, the immediate 4NT bid shouldn't be Keycard. But this is only theoretical. You and partner must agree on this. It is the most common Keycard Blackwood mix-up, and every pair that plays Keycard should have this one down pat by now. (See also the Keycard Blackwood agreement recommendations on page 130.)

17. What does the jump to 3NT mean after a two-over-one?

West	North	East	South
1 ♠	pass	2 ◊	pass
3 NT = 16-17			

West	North	East	South
1 ♠	pass	2 ◊	pass
2 ♡	pass	3 NT = 16-17	

Even diehard "fast arrival" players these days play that the jump to 3NT in these two auctions shows about 16-17 points. This meaning helps you to reach slam when there is a combined 33 points between you and partner but no trump fit.

18. If you use Jacoby 2NT, do you play the rebid at the four level as a void or a second suit?

West	North	East	South
1 ♠	pass	2 NT	pass
4 ◊ = void or 5-5?			

Also, here's another case for "slow arrival." We use the jump to 4♠ to show a balanced 14-15 points with strong trumps rather than a minimum.

19. After a 1NT response:

West	North	East	South
1 ♠	pass	1 NT	pass
2 NT	pass	?	

Is a suit at the three level forcing? Some say yes, some say no, some say only in hearts (our choice). Take your pick.

The cuebid as a limit raise:

20. After their overcall, most play weak jump raises with the cuebid as a limit raise or better:

West	North	East	South
1 ♠	2 ◇	3 ◇ = limit raise or better	

The only drawback is that South can now double to show a diamond honor. We prefer the jump to 3♠ here as limit and the cuebid as a slam try.

Minor-Suit Openings

21. After you rebid 1NT, do you play checkback? If so, is it always 2♣ or is it always the other minor? And have you discussed this sequence:

West	North	East	South
1 ♡	pass	1 ♠	pass
1 NT	pass	?	

22. After you rebid 2NT, do you play a checkback Stayman?

West	North	East	South
1 ♣	pass	1 ♠	pass
2 NT	pass	3 ♣ = checkback	

If you want to play checkback, the popular method of 3♣ is usually best (regardless of the opening bid), but then how do you show clubs? You'd better discuss the entire structure.

We don't play checkback, so we don't have these headaches. We might miss a 5-3 fit occasionally, but we maintain the ability to support partner's club suit (or show a club suit if partner opened 1◇). On the auction shown, East, with strong club support, may want to fish for slam without going past 3NT.

23. What is the jump to 2NT or 3NT after a minor-suit opening?

West	North	East	South
1 ♣	pass	2 NT = ?	

The trend today is toward a nonforcing 2NT response, with 3NT showing 13-15. We still play 2NT forcing (good 11 to 15) and 3NT as a strong notrump (16-17). With 18-19, we jump to 2NT and then bid 4NT over partner's raise to 3NT.

24. Do you play secondary jumps not forcing (popular) or forcing (our preference)?

West	North	East	South
1 ♣	pass	1 ♡	pass
1 ♠	pass	?	

East may jump to 2NT, 3♣, 3♡ or 3♠. Decide which of these bids is forcing, if any. (The reason we prefer them forcing is that it makes the bidding easier on game and slam hands. We jump with a limit raise or better and sometimes get overboard, but we never miss a game.)

The bottom line is this: Play them all forcing or all not forcing.

25. How high is "fourth-suit forcing" forcing to?

West	North	East	South
1 ♣	pass	1 ♡	pass
1 ♠	pass	2 ◊ = ?	

Many are now playing "fourth-suit forcing" to game. We play that if opener rebids at the two level, East can pass. And if East rebids at the two level or rebids 3◊, West can pass. No matter how you play it, East's next bid of 3♣, 3♡ or 3♠ is forcing.

26. What does the jump in the fourth suit mean?

West	North	East	South
1 ♣	pass	1 ♡	pass
1 ♠	pass	3 ◇ = ?	

Many play this as a weak 5-5! We play it forcing and with a weaker hand, we start with 2◇ over 1♠ and rebid 3◇. You decide.

27. How do you make a balanced game raise of responder's suit?

West	North	East	South
1 ♣	pass	1 ♠	pass
4 ♠ = ?			

Most play that this is the balanced, highcard point, raise. With distribution you jump to 4♣ with a two-suiter in clubs and spades, or make a splinter bid into a red suit.

Minor-Suit Raises:
28. After an inverted raise, where can you stop below game?

West	North	East	South
1 ♣	pass	2 ♣	pass
?			

One method: Opener or responder can get out at 2NT or three of the minor only on his second bid.

If you play inverted, do you play it if second seat overcalls? Most don't.

Do you play inverted by a passed hand? Most don't.

29. If you play limit raises in the minors, how do you make a forcing raise?

West	North	East	South
1 ◇	pass	3 ♣ = strong in diamonds	

Many play the jump to the other minor as an artificial forcing raise. This method is called "criss-cross."

30. After a reverse, do you know what is forcing on the next round?

West	North	East	South
1 ◇	pass	1 ♠	pass
2 ♡	pass	?	

Does West promise another bid?
Most say yes, unless East jumps immediately to game.

Can East drop West in his next bid? Maybe. The popular method is for East to bid 2NT with a weak hand (or the fourth suit, or rebid his suit with five of them, whichever is cheapest), and this is a warning to opener that he may be dropped. For example:

West	North	East	South
1 ◇	pass	1 ♠	pass
2 ♡	pass	2 NT	pass
3 ◇ = can be passed			

31. After a takeout double, third seat does not have to redouble with a good hand; he can pass and then later double for penalty.

West	North	East	South
1 ♠	double	pass	2 ◇
pass	pass	double = absolute penalty	

Passed-hand jumps:

32. What does a jump shift mean by a passed hand?

West	North	East	South
pass	pass	1 ♣	pass
2 ♡ = ?			

Many play the jump shift as fit-showing and forcing one round. This means West will hold a maximum pass with five hearts and at least four cards in clubs. Others play that the jump is not forcing and just promises a maximum pass. A third way to play is that the jump shows any maximum two-suiter (it could be a fit), and if East wants to hear the second suit, he should keep the bidding open with a forcing 2NT.

Still others play different meanings after a minor-suit opening and a major-suit. Some play splinter bids over major suits. And Drury players usually play the jump to 3♣ over a major as a maximum hand, six-card suit, not forcing. Choose your methods and come out agreeing.

Weak Two-Bids

33. When LHO doubles your weak two-bid, partner can bid a new suit or jump in a new suit as a lead-director and a fit. Some play only one of these bids shows a fit, some play both.

West	North	East	South
2 ♠	double	?	

3 ♢ = I have a raise to 3♠ but want you to lead a diamond if South declares.

4 ♢ = same as above but a raise to 4♠

34. In the sequence above, what does it mean if East bids 2NT or redoubles?

35. We play that the jump to 4♣ over a weak two-bid is Keycard Blackwood:

West	North	East	South
2 ♡	pass	4 ♣ = Keycard Blackwood in hearts	

  Ogust switch

If you use Ogust rebids after the 2NT response to a weak two-bid, you may want to fix your rebids by switching the meanings of 3◊ and 3♡. Many knowledgable partnerships have been playing the correct way for decades:

West	North	East	South
2 ♠	pass	2 NT	pass
?			

Standard Ogust Rebids:	The Correct Way:
3 ♣ = bad hand, bad suit	no change
3 ◊ = bad hand, good suit	good hand, bad suit
3 ♡ = good hand, bad suit	good suit, bad hand
3 ♠ = good hand, good suit	no change

This allows responder to show a heart suit over 3◊ when opener has a good hand but a bad spade suit. (When opener has a good suit, he rebids three of a major, and responder isn't as concerned about playing the other major.)

This switch also permits you to play the response of 3♡ over 2♠ as invitational, rather than forcing.

The way to remember this is: With bad suits, rebid a minor.

36. Can you correct the jump to 3NT over a weak two-bid? Or must opener pass on all hands?

West	North	East	South
2 ♠	pass	3 NT	

West	North	East	South
2 ♠	pass	2 NT	pass
3 any	pass	3 NT	

One of these auctions says that West must pass; one of them says that West can choose between 3NT and 4♠. The first auction is usually the shutout bid, but you could play the reverse. You decide.

Opening Preempts

37. Is a new suit forcing after you preempt at the three level?

Most say yes. We play forcing only when vulnerable. We also play the Roth convention that a bid of 4♣ over a three-bid shows a slam try in opener's suit.

38. After the opening bid of 4♡ or 4♠, what does a new suit mean?

West	North	East	South
4 ♡	pass	4 ♠ = ?	

Many partnerships play that a new suit is an asking bid. Responder may have a strong hand with two or more small cards in the suit bid. We prefer to play that a new suit is natural, correcting the contract. How would you like to pick up:

♠ A K Q J 10 x x x   ♡ —   ◊ Q J 10 9   ♣ x?

Suddenly partner opens 4♡ and you are playing that new suits are asking bids! Asking bids are scientific, but they also help the opening leader. Nevertheless, an asking bid may work wonderfully. You should decide. One compromise is to play asking bids only at the five level, keeping four of a major as natural. (This last idea is certainly best if partner opens with a four-of-a-minor preempt.)

Strong 2♣ Openings

39. After a strong artificial 2♣, what is your double negative? Most play "cheaper minor;" you start with 2◊ and then bid 3♣ over either major by opener or 3◊ over 3♣. On the horrible auction, 2♣-2◊; 3◊-?, you might want to play 3♡ as the double negative.

Many play a direct "double negative" and "general positive" over 2♣ (using 2◊ and 2♡ as artificial responses). We don't because we don't want to mess up the auction when opener has a 2♡ rebid.

40. After LHO overcalls our 2♣ opening, what is double by responder?

West	North	East	South
2 ♣	2 ♠	double	

The popular method today is that double is a terrible hand, saying nothing about the suit that is doubled. We prefer the old-fashioned penalty double, with a trump stack (by both responder and opener). Your choice.

Negative Doubles

41. Does a negative double promise four cards in the other major?

West	North	East	South
1 ◊	1 ♠	double	

Most say yes.
We agree.

42. Does a negative double promise both majors if both minors were bid?

West	North	East	South
1 ◇	2 ♣	double	

Most say no.

Support Doubles

43. Those who play support doubles (we don't) must clear up whether they play them over a one-notrump overcall.

West	North	East	South
1 ♣	pass	1 ♠	1 NT
double = ?			

Does this show three-card spade support or is it a penalty double?

Responsive Doubles

44. After partner overcalls or makes a takeout double, and third seat raises opener, a double is takeout.

West	North	East	South
1 ♠	2 ◇	2 ♠	double = takeout
1 ♠	double	2 ♠	double = takeout

Note: We play this double is penalty after partner makes a *takeout double* (second auction above), on the theory that partner has already doubled for takeout and we have a greater chance of having a trump stack in their suit. (As you can tell by now, we hate to lose the penalty double, which is why we play many doubles for penalty that others play for takeout.)

1NT Overcalls

45. Everybody plays "System ON" (or "Front of Card") these days, responding just as if partner had opened 1NT. Then what is a transfer into opener's suit?

West	North	East	South
1 ♡	1 NT	pass	2 ◇

You could play 2◇ here as natural, as a transfer to hearts (despite the opening bid!) or you could play it as a singleton heart with a further description to follow. Choose one.

46. Is "System ON" after a balancing 1NT overcall?

West	North	East	South
1 ♡	pass	pass	1 NT
pass	?		

So you don't forget, we suggest you play that System is always ON.

47. What about after they open a weak two-bid?

West	North	East	South
2 ♡	2 NT	pass	?

3 ♣ = Stayman
3 ◇ = singleton heart, without four spades
3 ♡ = transfer
3 ♠ = minors, at least two cards in hearts

Again, play System ON with the transfer into their suit showing a singleton in their suit and a minor-suit game or slam try.

This structure also applies when South balances with 2NT.

48. Do you play that 1NT is strong after they've made two bids?

West	North	East	South
1 ♣	pass	1 ♡	1 NT = ?

Many pairs play this as takeout for the other two suits (5-5). This is known as the "sandwich notrump." We still prefer the natural meaning, a strong notrump.

49. While we're on the topic, what does the fourth-seat cuebid mean?

West	North	East	South
1 ♣	pass	1 ♡	2 ♣ or 2 ♡ = ?

There is no consensus on this. We suggest that both "cuebids" be played as natural suits. West might have opened on a short suit or East may have a weak one. If you play the sandwich notrump, you certainly don't need a cuebid as well. If you play the one-notrump overcall here as natural, you may want to use the cuebid in the minor as takeout and the cuebid in the major as natural. You decide.

50. After a takeout double, a similar sequence occurs.

West	North	East	South
1 ♣	double	1 ♡	?

Here North has shown hearts, and there is the added possibility that East is psyching. Again, no consensus exists. We suggest:

double = good hand with 4+ hearts
2 ♡ = bad hand with 4+ hearts
2 ♣ = cuebid

Overcalls in Suits

51. After you overcall, is partner's cuebid ambiguous or does he promise a fit?

West	North	East	South
1 ♣	1 ♠	pass	2 ♣ = usually a spade fit

Most play the cuebid is ambiguous but usually South has a fit, and you assume so until you hear otherwise (e.g., he rebids a new suit). You rebid your suit with a weak overcall, otherwise bid naturally.

52. Many play the jump raise as preemptive and the cuebid as a "Mixed Raise," showing a preempt to the three level in your suit but with values.

West	North	East	South
1 ♣	1 ♠	pass	3 ♠ = preemptive

West	North	East	South
1 ♣	1 ♠	pass	3 ♣ = good preempt to 3♠

We play the jump raise as invitational to game, not a preempt, because we don't like to cuebid and allow opener to make a lead-directing double or slip in a new suit.

53. After partner overcalls, is your jump in a new suit forcing or invitational?

West	North	East	South
1 ♣	1 ♠	pass	3 ♡

Is 3♡ forcing or invitational? Choose one.

54. Most play that a passed-hand jump in a new suit is fit-showing, 10 cards between this suit and partner's suit. This is similar to #32 (page 120), where the jump is over partner's third- or fourth-seat opening bid.

West	North	East	South
pass	pass	1 ◇	1 ♠
pass	3 ♣ = clubs and spades		

55. When they double our cuebid, what should the overcaller do?

West	North	East	South
1 ♣	1 ♠	pass	2 ♣
double	?		

Most play that 2♠ is still the weakest action. Redouble shows a good hand and pass shows an average overcall without a new suit.

We prefer to play that pass is always the weakest call.

The Jump Cuebid

56. This is a strange cuebid. In the majors, everyone plays that it asks for a stopper for 3NT. But what about in the minors?

West	North	East	South
1 ♡	3 ♡ = solid minor, asking for a heart stopper		

West	North	East	South
1 ♣	3 ♣ = ?		

Most play it is a natural preempt (in diamonds as well). Make sure you and partner agree.

Against Weak Two-Bids

57. What is a cuebid of their weak two-bid?

West	North	East	South
2 ♠	3 ♠ = ?		

Most play it's asking for a stopper for 3NT, some play it's Michaels. You might also want to define a jump cuebid (4♠) and the jump to 4NT by North.

58. Many pairs play the jump to 4♣ or 4◇ over a weak two-bid as a strong two-suiter, showing the bid minor and the missing major:

West	North	East	South
2 ♠	4 ♣ = clubs and hearts		

We play that 4♣ is natural, showing only clubs. But if you play that it shows two suits, you should play the direct cuebid (#57) to ask for a stopper, since you no longer need a Michaels cuebid.

59. If you play lebensohl after weak two-bids, you will want to discuss the "slow shows" and "direct denies" features of this convention, similar to #8 over a 1NT opening (page 110). The difference here is that "slow shows" refers to showing four cards in the other major. Decide also if lebensohl is ON after a balancing double.

West	North	East	South
2 ♠	double	pass	?

2NT followed by 3♠ = shows four hearts but denies a stopper
2NT followed by 3NT = shows four hearts and a stopper
3NT direct = denies four hearts but shows a stopper
3♠ direct = denies four hearts and denies a stopper

To remember these bids:
(1) If you land in 3NT, you must have a stopper.
(2) Starting with 2NT Shows four cards in the other major.

60. Do you play responsive doubles after weak two-bids?

West	North	East	South
2♠	double	3♠	double = ?

Most play responsive. We prefer penalty if partner has made a takeout double, but responsive if partner overcalls. Someone once suggested South's double show specifically four cards in hearts. Choose one of these ideas and stick with it.

Slam Bidding

Roman Keycard Blackwood:

61. Most play that when in doubt, the last suit bid is the trump suit.

West	North	East	South
1♠	2♡	3♢	3♡
4 NT = RKB, diamonds agreed			

We prefer this: Four notrump is Keycard Blackwood only if a suit has been bid and raised, without exceptions.

62. Some play that 4NT is Keycard if a suit has been agreed, or it's for the last-bid suit when there is no longer any room to agree. Thus:

West	North	East	South
4♠	pass	4 NT = Keycard for spades	

West	North	East	South
1♠	2♡	3♢	pass
4 NT = simple Blackwood			

Your partnership should choose one method: (a) last-bid suit; (b) must agree; or (c) mixture. Choice (c) may be theoretically best but is the most likely to cause a mix-up. Choose your poison.

63. What does the Keycard Blackwood bidder's rebid of 5NT mean?

West	North	East	South
1 ♠	pass	3 ♠	pass
4 NT	pass	5 ♡	pass
5 NT = ?			

Does 5NT promise partnership possession of all the keycards and the queen of trump?

Almost everyone says yes.

Does 5NT ask for specific kings or the number of kings (excluding the trump king)?

Most prefer specific. We play number. You choose.

64. How do you show a void as responder?

West	North	East	South
1 ♠	pass	3 ♠	pass
4 NT	pass	?	

5 NT = two keycards plus a void

6 any = one keycard plus a void here

6 trump suit = one keycard plus a void in a higher suit

Cuebids:

65. Is your first slam try a cuebid or a suit?

West	North	East	South
1 ♠	pass	3 ♠	pass
4 ◇ = cuebid or suit?			

Most play it is a cuebid. We prefer suit. Either way it's a slam try. But what if West bids 4♡? Many play this not forcing.

66. After you cuebid, does partner have to cuebid with a weak hand and a control? Or does his cuebid also show extra values?

West	North	East	South
1 ♡	pass	3 ♡	pass
4 ♣	pass	4 ◇ = diamond control	

Most play that the "return cuebid" under the game level does not show anything but that control. But if East had bid above the game level (e.g., 4♠), he would promise extra values or a hand that has increased in value because of West's 4♣ bid.

67. What happens when your cuebid is doubled?

West	North	East	South
1 ♠	pass	3 ♠	pass
4 ♣	pass	4 ◇	double
?			

Most play that 4♠ is the weakest action. Redouble shows second-round control or better, and pass shows that West is still interested but cannot redouble.

We play that pass is our weakest call. This is a consistent theme in our competitive bidding, so we can never forget or have a mix-up. Nevertheless, you can play either way. Choose one method.

Forcing Auctions:

68. A related topic is "Forcing Auctions" after they take a sacrifice against your game. What constitutes a "Forcing Auction" is a subject in itself and a very difficult one at that. For example, many partnerships play that when your side bids a game and the opponents sacrifice at favorable vulnerability, the auction is forcing.

West	North	East	South
1 ♠	3 ♦	4 ♠	5 ♦
?			

If East-West are vulnerable and North-South are not, we have a forcing auction. West can pass and East must double or bid. Using the "favorable vulnerability" rule, at any other vulnerability this wouldn't be a forcing auction, and 5♦ could be passed out.

Change one bid, however, and we would have a forcing auction at all vulnerabilities:

West	North	East	South
1 ♠	3 ♦	4 ♦	5 ♦
?			

Now East has declared a strong hand and the auction is forcing. Five diamonds cannot be passed out.

> **Note:** There is a danger in playing the "favorable vulnerability" rule. Sometimes you want to bid a vulnerable game and you don't have much defense. For example:
>
> | West | North | East | South |
> |------|-------|------|-------|
> | 4 ♡ | 4 ♠ | 5 ♡ | ? |
>
> According to the rule, if East-West are favorable, South's pass is forcing. North may be looking at seven solid spades and out and South may have a complete yarborough, but the rule forces them to double a laydown 5♡ or go for a number in 5♠.

Let's assume you have established some guidelines for when an auction is forcing (see page 58 for a reasonable set of rules). Now what do your calls mean in these delicate situations?

69. In a forcing auction, most play the following system.

West	North	East	South
1 ♠	3 ◇	4 ◇	5 ◇
?			

a direct pass = no wasted values in their suit

a direct double = wasted values in their suit

a direct bid of the trump suit (5♠) = shortness in their suit and
   extra length in trumps, but not as strong as pass (if you pass
   and then pull partner's double, it shows a real slam try)

a direct new suit bid (5♡) = the same as 5♠ but shows hearts, too

We agree with this in general, but we play that the direct bid is
better than the direct pass, to be consistent with our competitive-
bidding rule that "pass is weaker than bidding."

The Special Case of Penalty Passes

70. When is pass for penalty? When your RHO redoubles and
you were planning to convert partner's takeout double for penalty.
But is partner on the same wavelength? He will be after you discuss
the following situation.

West	North	East	South
1 ♠	2 ♣	pass	pass
double	redouble	pass = Penalty, don't bid partner!	

This is the most typical case and we would guess that 100% of
America's 100 top partnerships have this case down to a T. East has
a trump stack and would have passed the balancing double if North
had passed. North may have his redouble or may be trying to screw
things up for East-West. In either case, he is about to go for a
number and West must pass and defend 2♣ redoubled unless he
wants to undermine his partnership.

There are many other cases, so we suggest this general rule:

Pass of a redouble is always for penalty except below the 1NT level when the passer is sitting in front of the potential declarer.

West	North	East	South
2 ♠	double	redouble	pass = penalty

South's pass is for penalty, so South must bid something if he does not want to convert the double. Two notrump could be used here as a takeout bid for two four-card suits.

West	North	East	South
1 ♠	double	redouble	pass = no meaning

South's pass has no meaning. The auction is below 1NT and South is sitting in front of the potential declarer.

West	North	East	South
1 ♠	pass	pass	double
redouble	pass = penalty		

North's pass is for penalty because he is sitting over declarer.

Some partnerships now play that the pass of 1♣ or 1♢ redoubled is also for penalty:

West	North	East	South
1 ♣	double	redouble	pass

You could play it this way if you like (it will prevent East from redoubling with a good hand and short clubs — or make him pay if he does redouble), but we prefer the rule above.

Two for the road

Here are two more interesting situations, which could lead to disaster if you don't have a good agreement.

1. Pass to play

Example Scenario: Your opponent opens 1NT and you have a decent 5-4-3-1 shape:

♠ A J x x x   ♡ K Q x x   ◊ K x x   ♣ x

Your system over 1NT is Landy. So you bid 2♣ and your LHO doubles. Now it goes pass, pass, back to you. Of course, you bid 2◊ and hope (pray) you can find a fit somewhere. But this time partner has seven clubs to the queen-jack and out! Your best spot was 2♣ doubled, but you land in your 3-3 diamond fit, down 1100. Where did you go wrong?

The solution is to play the "Pass to Play" treatment. The formula for remembering this is:

Whenever your artificial bid is doubled and your partner, who has never made a bid till now, passes, he wants to play it right there.

Memorize this rule, seal it and review it every month.

2. Redouble for rescue and redouble to play

In the last scenario, what would partner have done if he wanted you to choose a major? The answer is he would have redoubled. This is known as "redouble for rescue," and it's commonly used after one partner overcalls and gets doubled for penalty, or an opponent makes a penalty pass:

West	North	East	South
1 ◇	1 ♡	pass	pass
double	pass	pass	redouble = Help!

Nevertheless, there are many cases where you are doubled and you want to play redouble to say: "Don't run, partner. We're about to get rich!" They occur when:

(1) You open the bidding and the next hand doubles.

partner		*you*	
West	North	East	South
1 ◇	double	redouble = strength	

(2) One of you has shown strength and the other is using a convention, which is doubled.

partner		*you*	
West	North	East	South
1 NT	pass	2 ♣	double
redouble = let's play here			

(3) Whenever you bid game and get doubled.

partner		*you*	
West	North	East	South
1 NT	2 ♠	3 NT	double
pass	pass	redouble = happy here	

Some pairs, however, play that when 3NT is doubled, redouble expresses "doubt". We prefer to play redouble expresses "joy". You and partner must decide.

Chapter 14: Convention Check-List

Place a check next to each convention you want to play and have partner do the same. Order two martinis and come to some agreements. Asterisks (*) mean we highly recommend the convention.

☐☐Ace from Ace-King:* thru 4-level vs. suits/NT, not vs. preempts

☐☐Ace-Attitude, King-Count: lead vs. NT

☐☐Acol: English system, light openings, weak NT, limit bids

☐☐Acol Two-Bids: opening 2♡ or 2♠ to show an 8- or 9-trick hand

☐☐Asking Bids: asks for a control in that suit, often used over preempts

☐☐Astro: 1NT-2♣ = hearts and minor, 2◇ = spades and lower

☐☐Attitude Leads: vs. NT, the lower the spot the more you like it

☐☐Bart: 1M-p-1NT-p; 2♣-p-2◇ = artificial force

☐☐Bergen Raises: 1M-3♣ = 6-9 and 4-card support, 3◇ = limit raise

☐☐Better Minor: open better 3-card minor with no 5-card major

☐☐Blackwood:* simply asking for aces

☐☐Blue Team Club:* strong club system, step responses, 4-card majors

☐☐Brozel: 1NT-dbl. = any suit, 2m = m + H, 2♡ = H + S, 2♠ = S + m

☐☐California Cuebids: 1◇-1♠-2♠ = half of a stopper

☐☐Canapé: bidding shorter suit before longer

☐☐Cappelletti: 1NT-2♣ = any suit; 2◇ = Majors, 2M = that + minor

☐☐Checkback Stayman: 1m-p-1x-p; 1NT-p-2♣ = checkback

☐☐Choice-of-Games Cuebid:* e.g., 1♡-3◇-3♠-p; 4◇ = choose a game

☐☐Cole: opener's rebid of 2♣ shows several hand-types

☐☐Colorful Cuebid:* 1♠-2♠ = reds; 1♡-2♡ = blacks

☐☐Competitive Doubles: e.g., 1m-p-1M-overcall; p-p-double = takeout

☐☐Constructive Raises: 1M-p-2M = 8-10

☐☐Crash: 1♣ (16+)- dbl = 2 suits same <u>C</u>olor, 1N = <u>r</u>ank, 2♣ = <u>sh</u>ape

☐☐Criss-Cross: 1m-p-jump in other minor = game raise in first minor

☐☐Cuebids: Years ago showed the ace, nowadays can be the king

☐☐Dead Seat 2♣ or 2◇: 1m-p-1NT-p; p-cuebid of minor = majors

☐☐DONT: 1NT-double = C or D or H, 2m = that + higher, 2♡ = H + S

☐☐DOPI (or PODI), DEPO (or DOPE):* vs. Blackwood interference

☐☐Double Keycard Blackwood:* 2 suits are agreed, thus 6 keycards

☐☐Double Negative Cheaper Minor:* 2♣-p-2◇-p; 2M-p-3♣ = very weak

☐☐Drury (regular or reverse):* p-p-1M-p; 2♣ = Did you open light?

☐☐Exclusion Blackwood:* bid of void to ask for aces but not in that suit

☐☐Fit-Showing Jumps: e.g., p-1♠-2♡-2♠; 4♣ = clubs and hearts

☐☐Five Notrump Pick a Slam:* e.g., 1♡-3♠-4♣-5♠; 5NT = pick a slam

☐☐Five-Card Majors: 1M = 5+ in first or second seat

☐☐Flannery 2◇: Opening bid shows 4 spades and 5 hearts, 11-15

☐☐Flip-Flop: 1m-double-2NT = preempt in m; 3m = limit raise

☐☐Forcing Jump Raises:* 1 any-p-raise to 3 = game forcing

☐☐Forcing 1NT: 1M-p-1NT = unlimited; opener may rebid 3-card m

☐☐Four-Card Majors:* 1M opening = 4+; often played in 3rd position

☐☐Four-Notrump D.I.: e.g., 1♠-p-3♣-p; 4♣-p-4◇-p; 4NT = slam try

☐☐Four-Suit Transfers:* 1NT-p-2♠ = clubs, 2NT (or 3♣) = diamonds

☐☐Fourteen-Thirty Responses:* 4NT-p-5♣ = 1 or 4 keycards, 5◇ = 0 or 3

☐☐Fourth-Best Leads:* opening lead from 4-card suit or longer

☐☐Fourth-Suit Forcing:* e.g., 1◇-p-1♡-p; 2♣-p-2♠ = artificial force

☐☐Front of Card:* partner overcalls NT; respond as if he opened NT

☐☐Gambling 3NT:* opening bid to show solid minor

☐☐Gerber:* 4♣ asks for aces after partner opens NT or last bid is NT

☐☐Good-Bad 2NT: e.g., 1◇-1♠-double-2♠; 2NT = light 3-level bid

☐☐Grand Slam Force:* jump to 5NT asks about trump honors

☐☐Grano-Astro:* 1NT-double = spades + suit, 2m = that + hearts

☐☐Help-Suit Game Tries: 1♠-p-2♠-p; 3m = length, may be weakness

☐☐Inverted Minors: 1m-p-2m = limit raise or better, usually by UPH

☐☐Jack Denies, Ten Implies: lead vs. NT, 10=AJ10, KJ10, A109, K109

☐☐Jacoby Transfers:* 1NT-p-2◇ = hearts, 2♡ = spades

☐☐Jacoby 2NT: 1M-p-2NT = game force with support; opener bids sing.

☐☐ Jordan:* 1M-double-2NT = limit raise in M

☐☐ Jump Cuebids: e.g., 1♠-3♠ = asks pard to bid 3NT with spade stopper

☐☐ Kantar 3NT: opening 3NT to show long, solid major, no outside ace

☐☐ K-S System: Kaplan-Sheinwold, 5-card majors, 12-14 1NT

☐☐ Keycard Blackwood:* 5-ace response; the trump king = an ace

☐☐ Kickback: at 4-level, the suit above trump suit = Keycard Blackwood

☐☐ Kokish Relay: 2♣-p-2◊-p; 2♡ = hearts or 25+ balanced; 2♠ asks

☐☐ Landy:* 1NT-2♣ = majors

☐☐ Last Train Cuebids:* at 4-level, suit below trumps = art. slam try

☐☐ Lavinthal Discards: low = prefer lower suit; high = prefer higher

☐☐ Lead-Directing Pass: e.g., 2♠-3♡-p-3♠; pass = lead S; double = don't

☐☐ Lead-Directing Raises:* e.g., 3♡-double-4♣ = heart raise, lead a club

☐☐ Lebensohl: 1NT-2M-2NT = relay to 3♣, now any suit is competitive

☐☐ Lightner Double: dbl. of slam for dummy's first suit or "find my void"

☐☐ Limit Jump Raises: 1 any-p-raise to 3 = 10-11 points

☐☐ Mathe Over Strong Club: 1♣ (16+)-double = majors, 1NT = minors

☐☐ Maximal Game Tries:* e.g., 1♠-2◊-2♠-3◊; 3♡ = artificial game try

☐☐ Maximal Overcall Doubles:* e.g., 1♠-2♡-2♠-3♡; double = game try

☐☐ Mexican 2◊: opening to show 19-20 balanced

☐☐ Michaels Cuebid: 1m-2m = majors; 1M-2M = other M and minor

☐☐ Mini-Splinters: p-p-1M-p; 3 new suit = singleton, game try in M

☐☐ Minor-Suit Stayman:* 1NT-p-2♠ = good hand with minors

☐☐ Mixed Raises:* e.g., 1◊-1♠-p-3◊ = 7-9, good spade fit + singleton

☐☐ Multi-2◊: opening shows weak 2-bid in either major or strong hand

☐☐ Namyats: 4♣ opening = solid hearts, 4◊ = solid spades

☐☐ Negative Doubles:* double of overcall = takeout

☐☐ Negative Free Bids: e.g., 1♠-2◊-2♡ = not forcing

☐☐ Negative Slam Doubles: when a sacrifice looms, double = 0 defense

☐☐ New Minor Forcing: 1m-p-1M-p; 1NT-p-new minor = checkback

☐☐ New Suit 2NT:* 1 any-p-1 any-p; any suit rebid-p-2NT = forcing

☐☐ Nine Promises:* lead of the 9 vs. NT = one higher

☐☐ OBAR BIDS:* e.g., 1♡-p-2♣-2♠ = may be balancing prematurely

☐☐ Obvious Shift Signal:* at trick one, low card asks for obvious shift

☐☐ Odd-Even Discards: odd = encouraging, even = suit-preference

☐☐ Ogust:* 2M-p-2NT-p; steps to show suit quality and point range

☐☐ Pre-Acceptance:* e.g., 1NT-p-2◇ (transfer)-p; 2♠ = I love hearts!

☐☐ Precision System:* 1♣ = 16+, five-card majors, 13-15 notrump

☐☐ Precision 2◇: opening to show 4-4-1-4, 4-3-1-5, 3-4-1-5, 4-4-0-5

☐☐ Puppet Stayman: asks 5-card M; over 2◇, resp. bids M he doesn't hold

☐☐ Redouble for Rescue:* e.g., 1◇-2♣-double-p; p-redouble = help!

☐☐ Responsive Doubles:* 1♣-overcall or double-3♣-double = takeout

☐☐ Roman 2◇: opening to show strong hand and 4-4-4-1 shapes

☐☐ Roman Jumps: 2M-4m = that minor + the other major

☐☐ Rosenkranz Doubles: 1◇-1♠-2◇-double = spade raise + trump honor

☐☐ Roth 4♣ Over Preempts:* 3 any-p-4♣ = slam try in partner's suit

☐☐ Roth vs. 1NT: dbl = majors, 2m = that + spades, 3m = that + hearts

☐☐ Roth-Stone:* five-card major system with sound opening bids

☐☐ Rusinow Leads:* the lower of touching honors

☐☐ Sandwich Notrump: 1 any-p-1 any-1NT = 5-5 other two suits

☐☐ Serious 3NT (or Unserious): 1♠-p-3♠-p; 3NT = (un)serious slam try

☐☐ Short 1◇ Opening: used with Precision, may be 2 (or fewer)

☐☐ Short-Suit Game Tries: 1M-p-2M-p; new suit = singleton, game try

☐☐ Slow Shows (Direct Denies): lebensohl bids (see pages 110 and 129)

☐☐ Smith Echo: vs. NT, high-low in their suit = I like the opening lead

☐☐ Smolen: 1NT-p-2♣-p; 2◇-p-3M = five cards in other major

☐☐ Snap Dragon: e.g., 1♣-1♡-2◇-double = spades + tolerance for hearts

☐☐ Soloway Jump Shifts: 1m-p-jump shift = long suit or fit for minor

☐☐ South African Transfers: 1NT-p-4♣ = transfer to 4♡, 4◇ = tran. to 4♠

☐☐ Specific Kings after 5NT: 4NT-p-5 any-p; 5NT = bid a king, please

☐☐ Splinters:* 1M-p-double jump = 12-15 + singleton or void there

☐☐ Splinter Undisclosed:* 1M-p-3NT = any splinter; 4♣ asks where

☐☐ Stayman:* 1NT-p-2♣ asks for a four-card major

☐☐ Step Responses to 2♣: shows # of controls (ace = 2, king = 1)

☐☐ Suction: 1NT-overcall = next higher suit or the other 2 suits!

☐☐ Suit Preference at Trick One: signal at trick one: 10,9, or 8 for switch to higher suit; 7,6, or 5 continue suit led; 4, 3, or 2 asks for lower suit

☐☐ Suit Preference in Trump Suit:* high-low = I prefer a high suit

☐☐ Super Gerber: When 4♣ is natural, 5♣ is Gerber

☐☐Support Doubles: 1 any-p-1 any-overcall; double = 3-card support

☐☐Support Redoubles: 1 any-p-1 any-double; redouble = 3-card support

☐☐Swiss Raises: 1M-p-4♣ = 13-15 balanced raise, 4◇ = 16+

☐☐Switch:* e.g., 1◇-1♠-2♣ = hearts, 2♡ = clubs

☐☐System On: 1NT-double or 2♣-2 any = as if there'd been no double

☐☐Ten or Nine Shows 0 or 2 Higher: lead system vs. NT

☐☐Ten-to-Twelve One Notrump: usually 1st or 2nd chair, favorable

☐☐Texas Transfers:* 1NT (or 2NT)-4◇ = hearts, 4♡ = spades

☐☐Third from Even, Low from Odd: lead system vs. suits

☐☐Three Clubs Major Raise: 1M-p-3♣ = strong raise in M

☐☐Trump Echo for Count: high-low in trumps = odd number

☐☐Truscott Over Strong Club: overcall = that + next higher

☐☐Two Clubs After Takeout Doubles: 1M-double-2♣ = 8-9 raise in M

☐☐Two Diamonds Negative: 2♣-p-2◇ = negative

☐☐Two Diamonds Positive and 2♡ Negative: 2♣-p-2♡ = negative

☐☐Two Diamonds Waiting:* 2♣-p-2◇ = negative or no long suit

☐☐Two Spades Unknown Preempt: 2♠ opening = preempt in any suit

☐☐Two-Over-One Game Force: with less, respond 1NT forcing

☐☐Two-Way Checkback: 1m-p-1M-p; 1NT-p-2♣ = game inv., 2◇ = force

☐☐Two-Way Game Tries: e.g., 1♠-p-2♠-p; 2NT = help-suit game try
(responder relays to ask where), 3 of a suit = short-suit game try.

☐☐Two-Way Two-Bids: opening 2-bid = strong or weak in next higher

☐☐Unusual Notrump: 2NT overcall to show two lower unbid suits

☐☐Unusual Over Unusual:* 1M-2NT-3♣ = hearts, 3◇ = spades

☐☐Upper-Two Cuebid:* 1 any-cuebid = 2 highest unbid suits

☐☐Upside-Down Attitude: high = discouraging, low = encouraging

☐☐Upside-Down Count: high-low = odd #, low-high = even number

☐☐Walsh: 1♣-p-1M = may bypass longer diamond suit on weak hand

☐☐Weak Jump Overcalls: 1 any-jump overcall = weak, long suit

☐☐Weak Jump Raises: 1M-p-3M = weak

☐☐Weak Jump Shifts (or in comp):* e.g., 1♣-p-2♠ or 1♣-1◇-2♠ = weak

☐☐Weak Notrumps (12-14): In this system, the rebid of 1NT = 15-17

☐☐Weak Two-Bids:* 2◇, 2♡ or 2♠ openings, usually 5-11 points

☐☐Wolff Sign-Off: 1m-p-1M-p; 2NT-p-3♣ forces 3◇, then 3M = signoff

Chapter 15: What Does the Last Call Mean?

Two confusing and difficult areas of bidding involve doubles and early 4NT bids. Here are some auctions that are likely to cause a disaster unless you and partner are on the same wavelength. Jot your answers down on separate sheets, then compare notes.

	West	North	East	South
1.	West	North	East	South
	1 ♡	1 NT	pass	3 NT
	double			

	West	North	East	South
2.	West	North	East	South
	1 ♡	1 NT	2 ♠	3 NT
	double			

	West	North	East	South
3.	West	North	East	South
	2 ♠	double	pass	3 NT
	pass	pass	double	

	West	North	East	South
4.	West	North	East	South
	1 NT	pass	3 NT	double

	West	North	East	South
5.	West	North	East	South
	2 NT	pass	6 NT	double

	West	North	East	South
6.	West	North	East	South
	3 ♠	pass	6 NT	pass
	pass	double		

7. | West | North | East | South |
|------|-------|------|-------|
| 1 ♡ | 1 ♠ | 2 NT | pass |
| 6 NT | double | | |

8. | West | North | East | South |
|------|-------|------|-------|
| 3 ♠ | pass | 7 ♠ | double |

9. | West | North | East | South |
|------|-------|------|-------|
| 1 ♠ | pass | 3 ◇ | pass |
| 4 NT | pass | 5 ♠ | pass |
| 6 ♠ | pass | pass | double |

10. | West | North | East | South |
|------|-------|------|-------|
| 1 ♠ | pass | 3 ◇ | pass |
| 3 ♡ | pass | 4 ◇ | pass |
| 6 NT | pass | pass | double |

11. | West | North | East | South |
|------|-------|------|-------|
| 1 ♠ | pass | 1 NT | pass |
| pass | double | | |

12. | West | North | East | South |
|------|-------|------|-------|
| 1 ♣ | pass | 1 ♡ | pass |
| 1 NT | double | | |

13. | West | North | East | South |
|------|-------|------|-------|
| 1 ♣ | pass | 1 ♡ | pass |
| 1 NT | pass | pass | double |

14. | West | North | East | South |
|------|-------|------|-------|
| 1 ♣ | 1 NT | pass | pass |
| double | | | |

15. | West | North | East | South |
|------|-------|------|-------|
| 1 ♣ | pass | 1 ♡ | pass |
| 1 ♠ | double | | |

16. | West | North | East | South |
|------|-------|------|-------|
| 1 ♣ | pass | 1 ♡ | pass |
| 2 ♣ | double | | |

17. | West | North | East | South |
|------|-------|------|-------|
| 1 ♠ | pass | 1 NT | pass |
| 2 ♠ | double | | |

18. | West | North | East | South |
|------|-------|------|-------|
| 1 NT | double | 2 ◇ | double |

19. | West | North | East | South |
|------|-------|------|-------|
| 4 ♠ | double | | |

20. | West | North | East | South |
|------|-------|------|-------|
| 2 ♠ | double | 4 ♠ | double |

21. | West | North | East | South |
|------|-------|------|-------|
| 2 ♠ | 3 ♡ | 4 ♠ | double |

22. | West | North | East | South |
|------|-------|------|-------|
| 1 ♠ | 3 ♡ | 4 ♠ | double |

23. | West | North | East | South |
|------|-------|------|-------|
| 2 ♠ | double | 4 ♠ | 4 NT |

24. | West | North | East | South |
|------|-------|------|-------|
| 2 ♠ | 3 ♡ | 4 ♠ | 4 NT |

25. West	North	East	South
4 ♡	double	pass	4 NT

26. West	North	East	South
1 ♡	pass	4 ♡	double
pass	4 NT		

27. West	North	East	South
1 ♡	2 ♠	3 ◊	4 ♠
4 NT			

28. West	North	East	South
3 ♡	double	pass	4 NT

29. West	North	East	South
1 ♠	3 ♡	4 ◊	pass
4 NT			

30. West	North	East	South
1 ◊	4 ♡	4 NT	

31. West	North	East	South
1 ◊	4 ♣	4 NT	

32. West	North	East	South
1 ◊	double	1 ♡	4 ♠
4 NT			

33. West	North	East	South
1 ♣	4 ♡	4 ♠	pass
pass	double		

Popular Treatments, Alternatives and Rules for "What Does the Last Call Mean?"

Alert! We are now entering a very difficult area. We suggest that you and your partner study this chapter slowly. These auctions can create partnership disharmony if you don't have a firm agreement. The best way to handle them is by applying a general rule for similar-sounding auctions. Sometimes you have to weigh the "best possible meaning" against the "easiest to remember" and come up with a happy compromise. That's why we often give alternative rules; you should adopt the method best suited to you. Finally, please remember the golden rule that supercedes all others:

If the call you want to make could easily be misinterpreted by partner, don't make it.

---

1. West	North	East	South
1 ♡	1 NT	pass	3 NT
double			

Popular Treatment: Lead a heart.

We agree. In fact, it demands a heart lead. But what if the bidding had gone:

2. West	North	East	South
1 ♡	1 NT	2 ♠	3 NT
double			

The double still should ask for a heart lead.

Rule 1. The double of a notrump game says, "Lead my suit."

3. West	North	East	South
2 ♠	double	pass	3 NT
pass	pass	double	

Popular Treatment: Lead a spade.

Alternative: Don't lead a spade! East has a good hand with short spades. West should lead a heart or lead from minor-suit length.

Rule 2. The double of a notrump game says, "Don't lead your suit."

(This is consistent with Rule 1: Lead my suit.)

4. West	North	East	South
1 NT	pass	3 NT	double

Popular Treatment: Find my suit.

Alternative: A strong major, asking partner to lead his weaker major. If you have a strong suit, such as AKQxx, or KQJxx and an outside ace, your partner is not going to hold too much. Therefore, it is much safer to limit your lead-directing double to a choice of two suits rather than four suits. Even this method can backfire when partner has equal length in the majors or is longer in your major than the other.

Rule 3. With no suits bid by the defenders, the double of a notrump game asks for the first suit bid by dummy. If no suits were bid, double says, "Find my major."

If you're not happy with ambiguity, play the double for spades. This will permit you to make the following alternative rule:

Rule 3A. With no suits bid by the defenders, the double of a notrump game asks for the first suit bid by dummy. If no suits were bid, double says, "Lead a spade."

5. West	North	East	South
2 NT	pass	6 NT	double

Popular Treatment: No one knows.

Alternative: Lead a spade. This is consistent with rule 3A. It will also help partner when you have not doubled and he has a choice between a spade and another suit — he'll choose the other suit.

Rule 4. When no one has bid, the double of a slam asks for the highest ranking unbid suit.

This rule applies in all cases. Nevertheless, you may prefer to play differently. Check out these next few auctions and decide for yourself.

6. West	North	East	South
3 ♠	pass	6 NT	pass
pass	double		

According to rule 4, double asks for a heart lead. A spade lead probably isn't necessary if North has good spades. But if North has the ♡A-K, or ♡K-Q and an outside ace, a heart lead is vital.

7. West	North	East	South
1 ♡	1 ♠	2 NT	pass
6 NT	double		

Here is an even more confusing auction. Sticking to rule 4, however, the double asks for a diamond lead. If North wants a spade lead, he simply passes. If North wants a heart lead, it is unlikely to matter what South leads.

Leading against a slam is different from leading against a game, where partner may not want to lead his singleton in your suit. That's why the double of 3NT to demand your suit (rule 1) is necessary.

8. West	North	East	South
3 ♠	pass	7 ♠	double

Popular Treatment: Find my void.

Alternative: Lead a heart (rule 4). With a minor-suit void, simply pass, and North should lead a minor if he has length. Remember, this is just a sample auction; there are many similar auctions that can come up where you want to double a grand slam because you are looking at an ace or a void. If your double says "find my void," your partner may make a mistake or the opponents may escape successfully to notrump. But if your double calls for the "highest ranking unbid suit," partner can never go wrong and if you have the ace, the opponents can never escape.

9. West	North	East	South
1 ♠	pass	3 ♢	pass
4 NT	pass	5 ♠	pass
6 ♠	pass	pass	double

Popular Treatment: Lead a diamond.

Alternative: Lead a heart (rule 4). Isn't it likely that declarer needs the diamond suit to make his contract? Therefore, your diamond tricks won't go away. But he might be off two heart tricks or one heart and one trump trick.

The only case where the double for a diamond lead is crucial occurs when South is void in diamonds. And even then, the opponents may be able to run to 6NT successfully. Nevertheless, some of you may prefer to play the double for the first suit bid in dummy, in which case, we offer you an alternative to rule 4:

Rule 4A. The double of a notrump slam asks for the highest ranking unbid suit. The double of a suit slam asks for the first suit bid by dummy. If no suit has been bid by dummy, it asks for the highest ranking unbid suit.

10. West	North	East	South
1 ♠	pass	3 ◇	pass
3 ♡	pass	4 ◇	pass
6 NT	pass	pass	double

Here we have a case of three suits bid. What does that double ask for? With three suits bid, we use the following rule:

Rule 5. When three suits were bid by the opponents, the double of a slam asks for the third suit.

Therefore, in auction 10 above, double asks for a heart lead.

Doubles of 1NT:

11. West	North	East	South
1 ♠	pass	1 NT	pass
pass	double		

Popular Treatment: balanced 12-14 count.

Alternative: Penalty, lead a spade. The double here is very dangerous if you hold a random balanced 12-14 count, because partner is likely to be broke. Also, since the opponents have a misfit, your side may also have no fit. It is much safer, wiser, and occasionally very profitable to use the balancing double of 1NT for penalty, asking for the lead of the suit bid on your right.

12. West	North	East	South
1 ♣	pass	1 ♡	pass
1 NT	double		

Popular Treatment: takeout.

We agree. Here the double is made by the opening leader and, therefore, for takeout (diamonds and spades, possibly clubs as well).

13. West	North	East	South
1 ♣	pass	1 ♡	pass
1 NT	pass	pass	double

Popular Treatment: balancing, takeout.

Alternative: As before, penalty, asking for the lead of the first suit bid by dummy. If South had a takeout double, he probably would have made it on the first round of bidding. Thus, a good general rule for these doubles of 1NT is:

Rule 6. After an opponent opens the bidding one of a suit, the double of 1NT is: (1) takeout when you are on lead and (2) penalty when partner is on lead.

14. West	North	East	South
1 ♣	1 NT	pass	pass
double			

Popular Treatment: Penalty.

Alternative: Takeout for the majors. The odds on West being able to make a penalty double of 1NT are very small. But when West is short in diamonds with both majors, there is a good chance for a partscore or even a game. This balancing double of 1NT applies no matter what suit was opened. It always shows the majors.

Rule 7. The balancing double of a 1NT overcall shows the majors.

Second-Round Doubles of Suits:

15. West	North	East	South
1 ♣	pass	1 ♡	pass
1 ♠	double		

Popular Treatment: takeout, but confusing.

To clarify, the double is takeout of spades and permits you to play in clubs or hearts (the only cuebid South can make is spades). North might hold: ♠ x ♡ Q x x x ◊ K 10 x x ♣ A Q x x or stronger.

16. West	North	East	South
1 ♣	pass	1 ♡	pass
2 ♣	double		

Popular Treatment: confusion.

To clarify, this double is takeout of clubs and hearts (though it may include club length and probably includes heart shortness).

17. West	North	East	South
1 ♠	pass	1 NT	pass
2 ♠	double		

Popular Treatment: confusion.

Did North forget to double 1♠ for takeout? If not, is he now making a penalty double? Nothing is certain here, except one thing: For partnership harmony it's best to play consistently. We suggest that the double be takeout, 9-10 points with short spades.

Rule 8. The second-round double of any suit is takeout, even if you had a chance to double that suit earlier.

18. West	North	East	South
1 NT	double	2 ◊	double

Popular Treatment: Penalty.

Alternative: Takeout of diamonds, even if 2◊ means something other than diamonds. If South passes 2◊, North's reopening double is also takeout. This method covers all bases, whereas the penalty double covers only one situation. The following rule applies:

Rule 9. After the double of 1NT, the second double of the partnership is takeout. (The third is penalty.)

Four-level Problems:

19. West   North   East   South

     4 ♠   double

Popular Treatment: optional.

Now what does that mean? You can't have it both ways; either North is willing to hear partner bid a long suit or he isn't. We suggest you play the double for takeout in the usual sense, but the doubler can be more balanced than usual; partner is slightly less

 ## The Second-round overcall

This rare bird can have special meanings. In this day and age, it doesn't seem possible that a person will fail to overcall at the one level yet later overcall at the two level.

West   North   East   South

1 ♣   pass   1 ♡   pass

1 NT   2 ♠

What is 2♠? Did North overlook a card on the first round? You could play this way or you could play that North owns a club suit and this is the way he shows a spade-club two-suiter. Another idea is that North has a weak jump overcall in spades with four hearts and, therefore, didn't wish to bid 2♠ the first time. A third possibility is that North is trying to get doubled and has a solid spade suit! In any case, your partnership may want to define this overcall. Or perhaps this is a case for not defining the meaning, which gives you more leeway to trap the opponents.

likely to pull the double of 4♠ than the double of 4♡. The double shows "convertible values," not spade values.

If you and your partner both prefer penalty doubles of 4♠, by all means play penalty. But don't play "optional." This is just another word for the unethical two-way double that many club players unfortunately make (they double quickly for penalty and slowly for takeout or make some mannerism to suggest one or the other).

20. West	North	East	South
2 ♠	double	4 ♠	double

Popular Treatment: optional.

Alternative: Convertible values. The double should be values outside of spades, so North can bid a long suit if he has one. This is similar to auction 19 above. The downside of playing this way is that when you hold spade values, and you want to penalize them, you must keep a poker-face and pass. But this is much less likely to occur than the convertible-values hand-type.

Rule 10. Unless partner has preempted, the double of a 4♠ opening or raise shows "convertible values."

Rule 10A. The double of a 4♠ opening or raise is penalty.

Choose one of these: Rule 10 or 10A.

21. West	North	East	South
2 ♠	3 ♡	4 ♠	double

Popular Treatment: penalty (rule 10A).

Alternative: Values, same as before, allowing partner to bid a second five-bagger if he has one, or rebid 5♡ with extra shape. With a penalty double, again, you pass and simply take a smaller plus score or — on a happy day — convert partner's reopening double.

22. West	North	East	South
1 ♠	3 ♡	4 ♠	double

Popular Treatment: penalty (rule 10 or 10A).

We agree. Here North has preempted, so South has the final say.

> **Note:** Don't get confused between a preempt and a strong jump. Look at auction 21. If North jumps to 4♡ over 2♠, South's double is values, because the jump over a weak opening shows a strong hand. Now look again at auction 22. If North bids 4♡ over 1♠, South's double is still penalty, because 4♡ in that auction is a preempt.

23. West	North	East	South
2 ♠	double	4 ♠	4 NT

Popular Treatment: confusion.

Is it Blackwood or takeout? Our suggestion is takeout (for two suits, partner assumes minors until he hears otherwise).

Rule 11. 4NT over their 4♡ or 4♠ is takeout, unless we have agreed a suit or we are in a forcing auction.

Suggestion: On auction 23, if South rebids 5♡ over North's five-of-a-minor, it is a slam try in hearts (whereas the direct 5♡ would have been weaker).

24. West	North	East	South
2 ♠	3 ♡	4 ♠	4 NT

Popular Treatment: Keycard Blackwood for hearts.

Alternative: Takeout for two suits, or slam try in hearts. This auction is very similar to the last one, and the 4NT bid should again be takeout. Nevertheless, as we've said many times, agreement is more important than meaning. If you prefer to play it as Blackwood (or Keycard Blackwood for hearts), do so, and use the alternate rule:

Rule 11A. 4NT over their 4♡ or 4♠ is takeout, unless we are in a forcing auction or partner has bid a suit.

25. West	North	East	South
4 ♡	double	pass	4 NT

Popular Treatment: confusion.

If you apply rule 11, you are no longer confused. Since the opponent has bid four of a major, 4NT is takeout.

26. West	North	East	South
1 ♡	pass	4 ♡	double
pass	4 NT		

Popular Treatment: confusion.

This is the same as above, but illustrated to point out that it doesn't matter how they get to four of a major, your 4NT is takeout.

27. West	North	East	South
1 ♡	2 ♠	3 ♢	4 ♠
4 NT			

Popular Treatment: Blackwood.

We agree. If this constitutes a forcing auction for you (see rules for forcing auctions on page 58), West's pass would be forcing and, therefore, 4NT is Blackwood (rule 11 or 11A). Whether it's Keycard Blackwood for diamonds or simple Blackwood depends on your methods. (See agreements on Keycard Blackwood, page 130).

Since pass by West would be forcing, inviting East to bid, there's no need for West to make a takeout bid of 4NT.

28. West	North	East	South
3 ♡	double	pass	4 NT

Popular Treatment: confusion.

It could be Blackwood, takeout for minors or even natural (a strong notrump). We once spent an entire flight to a tournament in Iceland discussing this one sequence! Five hours later, we came up with this idea. After partner makes a takeout double of a preempt:

• the jump to 4NT is natural

• the cuebid shows a slam try (the cuebid followed by 4NT, given the chance, is Blackwood)

This is easy to forget, however, unless you, too, have spent an entire flight discussing it. So for practical purposes, we suggest:

Rule 12. The jump to 4NT is always Blackwood.

29. West	North	East	South
1 ♠	3 ♡	4 ◊	pass
4 NT			

Popular Treatment: Blackwood

Alternative: Natural, to play. West is endplayed in the auction anytime he holds five spades, no diamond fit and good hearts:

♠ K 10 x x x ♡ K J 10 x ◊ J x ♣ A Q

What a nightmare! And it would be worse if West held a singleton diamond. The guiding rule here is:

Rule 13. If partner's first natural bid is 4♣ or 4◊ and the next hand passes, 4NT is to play.

It has also been suggested that the cuebid of 4♡ by West, in auction 29, be Keycard Blackwood for diamonds.

West	North	East	South
3 ♡	4 ◇	pass	4NT = natural

The solution to this auction is the same as in auction 29.

30. West	North	East	South
1 ◇	4 ♡	4 NT	

Popular Treatment: Keycard Blackwood for diamonds.

Alternative: takeout. This is easy by now. If you have agreed on rule 11, this 4NT shows something like six clubs and three or four diamonds. But if East bids 5♠ (wow!) over West's 5♣, East may hold a real monster, such as: ♠ A Q J x x ♡ x ◇ A x ♣ K Q J x x. If you have agreed on rule 11A, 4NT is Keycard Blackwood.

31. West	North	East	South
1 ◇	4 ♣	4 NT	

Popular Treatment: Blackwood.

Alternative: Natural. This is a matter of taste. You can play it natural if you like, but then agree on the following rule:

Rule 14. When the opponent has preempted 4♣ or 4◇, and you have not agreed a suit and you are not in a forcing auction, 4NT is natural.

32. West	North	East	South
1 ◇	double	1 ♡	4 ♠
4 NT			

Popular Treatment: Blackwood.

Alternative: Takeout. South bid 4♠, so 4NT is takeout (rule 11). West may hold 0-3-6-4 shape. The point is you don't have to worry, if you have a good rule. (If you play rule 11A, 4NT is Blackwood.)

33. West	North	East	South
1 ♣	4 ♡	4 ♠	pass
pass	double		

Popular Treatment: optional, extra values.

Alternative: A desire to bid 5♡, plus defense. Optional is a terrible way to play this double, because East will never know when to pull it. We suggest North hold something like this:

♠ — ♡ A K Q J x x x x ◊ A x ♣ x x x

Rule 15. After you preempt to the four-level, your reopening double is takeout, showing shortness in their suit and extra length in your suit. Partner converts the double only with trump tricks. Otherwise, he bids.

You might think this is too rare and prefer to play the reopening double as penalty. This is certainly reasonable. North, in auction 34, might pick up:

♠ K Q J x ♡ A J 10 x x x x ◊ x x ♣ —

So you would apply this alternate rule:

Rule 15A. After you preempt to the four-level, your reopening double is penalty. You have a trump stack and you want partner to pass.

The reason we prefer rule 15 to 15A is that by playing for takeout we don't bid in front of partner (if you play double is penalty, you would be forced to bid 5♡ by yourself on the first example). Also, the double for penalty (second example) could backfire if East has bid 4♠ with a two-suiter in clubs and spades.

Epilogue

Epilogue: It Happened One Night

Matthew: Well, it's near the end of another book and, as usual, I feel like there's so much more to say.

Pamela: Don't hold yourself back. I have my red pencil with me.

Matthew: OK. One of the topics we've touched on but haven't really discussed enough is stress. You know the kind I mean — when one partner can't make the bid or play he wants because the other is going to get annoyed if it backfires. This is especially the case with married partnerships, though it applies to everyone. As Larry said in his "Love Thy Partner" chapter, bridge partnerships are a lot like marriages.

Pamela: Marriages are made in heaven, dear. Bridge partnerships come from a lower place.

Matthew: Well, I thought we'd have a look at the darker side of partnership bridge — the emotional stress of having to play perfectly on every single hand.

Pamela: If you can't take the pressure, perhaps you should . . .

Matthew: Thank you. I'd like you to take a look at the following hand, which came up at the European Team Championships of 1997. With nobody vulnerable, you are in fourth seat with:

♠ A K 10 6 3 2 ♡ 6 2 ◇ Q J 6 4 3 ♣ —

The dealer on your left opens one heart. It goes pass by partner, one spade on your right. What is your call?

According to our recommendation (see page 126) the best bid is 2♠. This is a natural overcall. Let's assume that your partnership has agreed on this meaning and you overcall 2♠. Now a surprising thing happens. Your LHO jumps to four spades! Two passes to you and you are left with this intriguing problem:

West	North	East	South
—	1 ♡	pass	1 ♠
2 ♠	4 ♠	pass	pass
?			

Your choices now are:
pass
double

Which would you choose? (Cowards, beware. Do not turn the page until you make your decision. But before you do, I invite you to read a brief analysis of the situation.)

Analysis

Let's look at the upside and downside of these two calls. First we have pass, a chicken call if I ever saw one. Perhaps South has bid a three-card suit, perhaps North has raised to game with three trumps. In either case, you are in a position to enjoy a huge set by doubling. And if you don't double, you may very well become the laughing stock of your team, the tournament, and the entire bridge-reading population. "Always make an obvious double," a great player once advised. "The opponents never run."

On the other hand, what if the opponents are having an accident? Could North have pulled the wrong bidding card out of the bidding box? Could he have missorted his cards? Or could he have meant his four-spade bid as some sort of weird cuebid? But without a fit? Forcing to the five level after opening at the one level?

Anything is possible in this crazy game, and there is that "Bird in Hand" philosophy — take the sure plus and all that sort of thing. If you double and they run to a better spot, partner is not going to like it, your teammates are not going to like it, even your psychiatrist is not going to like it.

Now let's look at the partnership aspect of this one. As I said, no matter what you do, if it's wrong, partner's going to be unhappy. If you pass and collect 200 at 50 a trick, he (in my case, she) is going to say, "You need seven trumps to double?" But if you double and they run to a makeable spot, your partner will say, "Very clever. You overcalled a natural 2♠ and you think your opponents are nuts enough to bid game in your suit?" Of course, Larry Cohen would say that partner won't (or shouldn't) say a word. Oh no, after you make the spectacularly wrong decision, partner will sit there like Hamman or Wolff bobbing his head unemotionally, continuing on to the next board pleased as punch to be sitting opposite a nincompoop.

Now that we've sorted out the possibilities, what is your call?

Pamela: Just a minute. You're all emotionally wound up, as usual. Why don't you simply consider the consequences of your actions? This is a bridge problem. If the opponents are in the wrong contract, you're about to get a good score. Should you risk a good score for a great one at the cost of disaster? Of course not. You simply pass, and if anyone calls you chicken, you cluck your way to the bank. This is not a macho contest, this is a game of logic.

Matthew: If this were a game of logic, would my opponents be in four spades missing six of them to the ace-king? All right, let's suppose you pass (though I think you should stand on your chair and scream it — this could be the case of the "stand-up pass"). Now let's suppose the full deal is something like this:

South dealer   North
Everybody tense   ♠ Q 9 8 4
            ♡ A K 10 5 3
            ◇ A K
            ♣ K 7

West (you)   East
♠ A K 10 6 3 2   ♠ —
♡ 6 2   ♡ Q J 7 4
◇ Q J 6 4 3   ◇ 8 7 5 2
♣ —   ♣ Q J 10 8 6

            South
            ♠ J 7 5
            ♡ 9 8
            ◇ 10 9
            ♣ A 9 5 4 3 2

West	North	East	South
—	1 ♡	pass	1 ♠
2 ♠	4 ♠	(all pass)	

After three rounds of spades, declarer takes six tricks. As predicted, +200 to East-West. You put your cards quickly in the board and your partner says, "How many spades did you have?" or "Did we beat that three or four?" or "May I see your hand?"

Pamela: The main theme of this book is that partner shouldn't say any of these things. (Anyway, North might beat East to the punch on these questions.) Also, if you were East in a rubber bridge game and went plus 200 with those cards, should you complain? You'd be happy. And that's why West must pass — because even if he's wrong, he'll go plus.

I think it's time to see the real hand:

South dealer   North
None vul   ♠ —
                    ♡ A K Q 10 3
                    ◇ A 10 9 7
                    ♣ K Q 7 6

West   East
♠ A K 10 6 3 2   ♠ Q 9 8
♡ 6 2   ♡ J 7 5
◇ Q J 6 4 3   ◇ K 8 5 2
♣ —   ♣ J 10 8

                    South
                    ♠ J 7 5 4
                    ♡ 9 8 4
                    ◇ —
                    ♣ A 9 5 4 3 2

West	North	East	South
—	1 ♡	pass	1 ♠
2 ♠	4 ♠	pass	pass
double	4 NT	pass	5 ♣
pass	6 ♣	pass	7 ♣
(all pass)			

Pamela: This is the real story. West doubled and North-South got back on track. Instead of going +300 (4♠ undoubled, down six), West went minus 1440 (7♣ making).

Matthew: Yes, you were right, pass was the winning call, but that's not my point. I ask you to assume the position of East on this deal (the only innocent player at the table). Assume that your partner of long-standing was sitting West and made this costly double. How would you handle the situation?

Pamela: To be honest, before writing this book I would have

said something sarcastic to West. (More likely I would quit bridge and find a hobby I could do on my own, like reviewing movies.) But I think after our work on this book, I'd be ready to steel myself to say nothing —

Matthew: No facial expressions?

Pamela: No anything. I would simply go on to the next board. I would try to think of this as a missed opportunity rather than a loss, and hope it's a push board.

Matthew: I believe you as long as your partner was anyone else but me. With me you'd be furious. This is why I'd be in a stressful position if I held the West cards. But if you held the West cards, you'd have no problem. Your partner allows you the complete freedom to do what you like and never criticizes. If you'd allow me the same freedom, maybe I'd be able to think more clearly and come up with the winning call more often.

Pamela: If you want freedom to do what you like, play chess. Look, maybe a bridge partnership is like a marriage. You marry someone who's suited to you in most ways and you form a bridge partnership with someone who also suits you 90% of the time. But there's no perfect spouse and there's no perfect partner. Both sides have to make some compromises along the way. And the main time for those compromises is when the stakes are high. At those difficult times, you have to do what your partner likes. Or, to put it a better way, paraphrasing the words of the golden rule ("Don't do to someone else what you do not like done to you."): Don't make the call or play that your partner won't be happy with.

Matthew: I would like follow this advice. But sometimes a guy is in a situation where he doesn't know how to make his partner happy.

The Last Word (Pamela): Then just remember who your partner is. On this deal, if I were East, you'd know that I'd be happy with a plus score, so you pass. If, however, you were playing with another sort, one of your cronies who can't stand missing a big set and doesn't mind the occasional disaster, you'd double — knowing that you were making the call that will please your partner.

As for relieving stress at the bridge table, I can think of one fool-proof idea: Let's stay home tonight and watch a good movie!

Partnership Principles

• In a crucial bidding situation, consider your partner, too. What will annoy him the most? Once you figure it out, don't do it.

• Taking a sure plus score is usually a good tactic.

• Don't cuebid at the four level in a suit partner has bid.

• To make a partnership work, you have to compromise a little. There are no two people who think exactly the same way about everything.

• Victor Mitchell once said, "Bridge makes fools of us all." When the inevitable disaster strikes, remember that perfection in bridge is impossible. Your partner has given you a lot of fine play over the years, so don't let the occasional error destroy your partnership.

• If you must say something after a disaster, perhaps the best thing is a simple "Forgive me, partner." If you can forgive and forget quickly, your partnership will flourish.